In the name of Allah
The Merciful, the Compassionate

Other books by the same author

Islam Rediscovered
The True Jihad
A Treasury of the Quran
The Quran for All Humanity
The Quran: An Abiding Wonder
The Call of the Qur'an
Words of the Prophet Muhammad
An Islamic Treasury of Virtues
Islam and Peace
Introducing Islam
The Moral Vision
Principles of Islam
Indian Muslims
God Arises
Islam: The Voice of Human Nature
Islam: Creator of the Modern Age
Woman Between Islam and Western Society
Woman in Islamic Shari'ah
Islam As It Is
Religion and Science
Tabligh Movement

THE PROPHET
Muhammad
A SIMPLE GUIDE TO HIS LIFE

MAULANA WAHIDUDDIN KHAN

Goodword

First published 2002
Reprinted 2013
© Goodword Books 2013

Goodword Books
1, Nizamuddin West Market
New Delhi-110 013
Mob. +91-8588822672
Tel. +9111-4182-7083, 4652-1511
email: info@goodwordbooks.com
www.goodwordbooks.com

Islamic Vision Ltd.
434 Coventry Road, Small Heath
Birmingham B10 0UG, U.K.
Tel. 121-773-0137
e-mail: info@ipci-iv.co.uk
www.islamicvision.co.uk

Non-Profit Bookstore
Talim-ul-Islam Community Center
86 Rivalda Road, Toronto ON M9M 2M8, Canada
Tel. 416-780-7844
email: lugatulquran@hotmail.com, www.LQToronto.com

IB Publisher Inc.
81 Bloomingdale Rd, Hicksville
NY 11801, USA
Tel. 516-933-1000
Toll Free: 1-888-560-3222
email: info@ibpublisher.com
www.ibpublisher.com

Printed in India

Contents

The Life of the Prophet

The Prophet of Islam, Muhammad ibn Abdullah ibn Abdul Muttalib, who was born in Makkah in 570 A.D. and died in Madinah in 632 A.D. received the prophethood at the age of forty. We give here a brief sketch of his life.

Muhammad ﷺ was still in his mother's womb when his father Abdullah died. A few years after his birth, his mother too passed away. In accordance with the ancient Arab custom, he was looked after by a Bedouin woman, Haleema Sadia. Being an orphan, he was taken charge of by his grandfather, Abdul Muttalib. After the latter's death, Muhammad's uncle, Abu Talib, who was a merchant, became his guardian. The Prophet accompanied him on certain trading journeys. At the age of twenty five he married a Makkan widow, Khadijah bint Khowailid, who was forty years old at the time.

When the Prophet was forty years old, he received his first revelation from God, in the cave of Hira near

Makkah, where he often used to go in search of solitude. It was here that the Angel Jibril came to him for the first time and gave him the good tidings that God had chosen him as His Prophet. The first few verses revealed to him on this occasion form part of chapter 96, titled 'The Clot' in the Qu'ran.

The Qur'an was not revealed in the form of a book, all at once, but in parts, very gradually over a period of 23 years. Extraordinary arrangements were made for the preservation of the Qur'an from the very first day of its revelation. Whenever any part of the Qur'an was to be revealed, Jibril would visit the Prophet and recite the relevant verses to him. He would first of all commit them to memory, then dictate them to his scribes, so that they could be preserved for posterity. The Prophet possessed an excellent memory, but being unable to read and write, he appointed a number of his companions as "transcribers of revelation." One or the other transcriber always remained in his company so that he could immediately write down the passages of the Qur'an as soon as they were revealed. The Prophet took such great care in this matter that even during such a critical and precarious journey as that of emigration, he was accompanied by a scribe, Abu Bakr. Along with other necessary items he always kept pen and paper with him in order that the revealed passages could be immediately recorded.

Another special arrangement made along with

their preservation in writing was the memorizing of the verses by most of the companions. These memorized verses were then recited daily in their prayers. In this way the preservation of the Qur'an was simultaneously being done in two foolproof ways.

When the entire Qur'an had been revealed, Jibril came to the Prophet and recited the entire scriptures from the opening chapter to the last, (titled 'Men,') in exactly the same order in which they exist today. The Prophet then recited the entire Qur'an in this revised order to his companions. A large number of them who had already memorised the entire Qur'an in its initial order, now adhered to the new arrangement. They used to recite the Qur'anic verses again and again in their daily prayers and at the same time read out passages to others.

In this way the Qur'an was compiled during the life of the Prophet, and to this day it has remained in the same form. Subsequently the first Caliph, Abu Bakr, had this compilation prepared in the form of a bound volume. Gradually, copies of it were circulated to all the provincial centres.

After Muhammad "received the prophethood, his lifestyle changed completely. He stopped going to the cave of Hira, and engaged himself fully in the communication of the message he had received from God. At that time, idolatry being prevalent in Makkah, the Prophet began to tell people that idolatry was the practice of empty rituals. The true religion was the worship of one God, obedience to His commands alone, and a life lived in accordance with His will. He stressed that the idolatrous religions would not be acceptable in the Hereafter; only to monotheism would any value be attached. The true monotheists would be rewarded by God with heaven in the Hereafter.

His method of propagating the true faith (*dawah*) consisted mostly of reciting a passage from a part of the Qur'an to the people (*madu*). Sometimes he would go to a place where people had gathered and would say: "O people, say there is no Being worthy of worship save God and you will be successful." In this way the Prophet continued to communicate the message of monotheism to the idolaters around him.

In the beginning the Prophet adopted the method of conveying the message privately to people at an individual level. About three years later he began publicly to invite people to accept monotheism. It was then that he met with opposition. At that time the Makkans as well as other tribes of Arabia had adopted idolatry as a religious practice. They apprehended that the Prophet wanted them to abandon the religion of their ancestors and follow a new religion. But this was something they could never tolerate. In that case it was but natural for them to oppose the message of monotheism.

Furthermore, there was another dimension to

idolatry for the Makkans. No economic resources or agriculture existed in Makkah. The only thing of value that it possessed was the sacred house built by Abraham and Ismail. The Makkan leaders had placed therein all the idols, numbering 360, which were worshipped by different Arab tribes. The Arabs would visit the Kabah all the year round to make offerings to these deities. Over and above this, the large gathering of pilgrims was also responsible for the flourishing of trade in Makkah. These were the two main reasons for the majority of Makkans becoming staunch opponents of the Prophet of Islam.

However, the serious-minded people of Makkah did not fail to realize the truth of his message, and gradually began to accept Islam. About 200 people from Makkah as well as the surrounding areas entered the fold of Islam after a 13-year period of *dawah* activity.

The Makkan leadership was in the hands of the Quraysh tribe. Such leaders as Abu Jahal, Abu Lahab, etc., turned hostile to the Prophet. First they wanted to stop the spread of the religion by opposing it. But very soon they realized that their opposition was ineffective. In the meantime, the Prophet's uncle, Abu Talib, died. He had been a leader of the Quraysh, and the Prophet's guardian and supporter.

After the death of Abu Talib the Makkan leaders intensified their opposition. They began openly indulging in hostile activities. At that time the Prophet, feeling that the situation in Makkah was not favourable for spreading his message, allowed his companions to temporarily leave Makkah and migrate to Abyssinia, a neighbouring country. As for himself he decided to go in search of supporters in an Arabian town, called Taif. He was accompanied only by his servant Zayd.

This journey did not yield any positive result. The leaders of Taif, turning against him like the Makkan leaders, treated him very badly. Therefore, the Prophet returned to Makkah. However, the support of a Makkan leader was necessary if he was to stay in the city. So when he was still on the outskirts of his home town, he sent his servant to the Makkan leader Mutim ibn Adi,–still an idolater,–with the request that he extend his patronage so that he might stay in Makkah. This protection was necessary according to the ancient Arab system. Only when Mutim ibn Adi agreed to do so was the Prophet able to enter the city. But now the opposition of the Makkan leaders had so greatly intensified that it had become impossible for him to stay there. Therefore, after thirteen years of Prophethood, he quietly left Makkah for Madinah.

After reaching Madinah the first sermon he gave at the Friday prayer has been recorded in full by his biographer, Ibn Hisham: After praising God, the Prophet said:

O people, prepare yourself for the Hereafter. You must know that the hour of death is sure to come to everyone. Then you will leave your herds without a herdsman. Then surely the Lord will speak to you. And then there will be no mediator, no veil to come between him and his Lord. The Lord will ask: Did My messenger not come to you? Did he not convey My message to you? I gave you wealth, and blessed you. Then why did you not prepare yourself for this day? Then that person will look towards his left, and towards his right, but he will not see anything. Then he will look in front of him, but he will see nothing but hell. Therefore, if any one of you is eager to save his face from the fire of hell he ought to do so, even if it is by giving a piece of a date (by spending in charity for those who are really in need). One who does not possess even that should try to save himself by speaking a good word. For each good action will be rewarded from tenfold to 700 fold. May God bless you. May God's mercy be upon you."

During the thirteen years that the Prophet lived in Makkah after he received prophethood, prayer in congregation had not been made obligatory. It was in Madinah, after his emigration, that congregational prayer was made a religious duty. Therefore, on reaching Madinah, the first of the most important tasks in which the Prophet engaged himself was to find a piece of land on which to build a mosque. The mosque he built has seen several extensions since then, and is now known as *Masjid-e-Nabawi.*

On the subject of mosques the Prophet observed: "The mosques are the home of the God-fearing." That is, the mosques are the training centres for a God-fearing life for the believers.

After the construction of the mosque, the Prophet stayed in a room adjacent to it. Here he organized congregational prayers to be said five times in the day: *Fajr* (dawn prayer), *Zuhr* (midday prayer), *Asr* (afternoon prayer) *Maghrib,* (after sunset prayer) and *Isha* (evening prayer). In addition to this, the Prophet established weekly prayer on Fridays. This prayer was congregational and wider in scope, for it included a sermon, a weekly discourse for the spiritual development of the believers.

In Madinah the Prophet undertook many tasks for the organisation and consolidation of the Muslim *ummah.* For instance, after the emigration the small town of Madinah saw, all of a sudden, the addition of several hundred people. This was a major social problem. For its solution the Prophet adopted a strategy known in Islamic history as 'fraternizing.' The form it took was a bond of brotherhood established between one Ansar (a Madinan Muslim) and a Muhajir (emigrant from Makkah). Each one of the emigrants was connected with a member of the Ansari Muslims in a bond of mutual assistance. The Ansaris shared their wealth and property with the Muhajirs as if they were the members of their own families. The Ansar and Muhajirs thus fraternized, living together like real brothers, without ever quarrelling over anything.

After some time, there was no further need for this fraternity. Since the Muhajirs did not feel comfortable in becoming a burden on others, they engaged themselves in different activities. Some took to farming, others to trade and yet others chose to labour in the fields owned by the Ansar. In this way after a very short period of time, everyone was able to stand on his own feet.

Madinah was also inhabited by some idolaters and Jews, who were in a minority. The Prophet decided that some form of law should be established so that there would be no misunderstanding or hostility of any sort, in the future between them and the Muslims. To solve this problem the Prophet of Islam issued a charter commonly known as the covenant of Madinah. Since the Muslims were in the majority, the Prophet's position became that of a leader, or a head of state. In this capacity he declared in this charter that all the inhabitants of Madinah would enjoy equal rights. Everyone would be free to follow the religion and culture of his or her choice: the affairs of the Muslims would be decided according to the shariah, while the affairs of the Jews and idolaters would be decided according to their traditions, laws and customs.

Unlike Makkah, Madinah proved to be very favourable to the Prophet's propagation of monotheism. Even prior to his coming to the town, Islam had already entered Madinah. After his arrival, the *dawah* process was intensified and the majority of the Madinan people accepted Islam, becoming his supporters.

This situation was not to the liking of the Makkans. They found it intolerable that someone they had expelled from Makkah should have found a stronghold in Madinah, for now the Prophet posed a far greater threat to their idolatrous religion. On the basis of this thinking, they decided to take military action against him. The religion they had failed to extirpate by simple opposition, they now resolved to wipe from the face of the earth by the sword.

After the emigration, therefore, the Makkan leaders opened hostilities. One of the skirmishes came to be known as "Badr the first." However, the first big armed confrontation, initiated by the Makkan leaders, took place, eighty five miles south-west of Madinah in 624 A.D. (2 A.H.), and is known as the Battle of Badr. With special divine succour the battle resulted in complete victory for the Prophet and his Companions. Seventy Makkans, most of them leaders, were killed and the same number were taken prisoner.

The defeat at Badr provoked the Makkan leaders more than ever. They incited the Makkans to do battle by saying that they had to avenge the killing of their people at Badr. (In ancient Arabia the avenging of killings was considered a sacred duty devolving upon the survivors). Consequently several skirmishes took place between the two parties. In the following year the Makkans under Abu Sufyan collected a large army and reached the borders of Madinah. The two armies engaged in a fierce battle near the Uhud mountain. The believers had actually won the battle but then, taking advantage of a mistake inadvertently committed by the Companions, the Makkans managed to charge again. The Muslims, confounded by this sudden attack, suffered great loss in terms of lives. The Prophet himself was wounded. The Makkans could avenge at Uhud their defeat at Badr.

The Prophet of Islam felt that war was not the solution. Therefore, he adopted another strategy. Guided by a dream, he announced in 6 A.H. that he intended to leave for Makkah in order to perform Umra, (circumambulation of the Kabah) and other rites. Accordingly, about 1400 of his Companions accompanied him. It was a peaceful march, with no military overtones.

Arrivals of such peaceful delegations were nothing new for Makkah. Various tribes of Arabia regularly used to come to visit the Kabah. But the Makkans could not tolerate this influx of Muslims, whom they considered their bitterest enemies. When the Prophet reached a place called Hudaybiya, while still on the march, the Makkan leaders objected to his advancing any further. They felt it was damaging to their prestige that the very people who had been expelled by them from Makkah should come to the city again and perform the rights of Umra openly and in such large numbers.

Now the Prophet halted at Hudaybiya and began negotiating for peace with the Makkan leaders. Finally, after lengthy parleys an agreement was reached which came to be known as the Treaty of Hudaybiya. In this, the Prophet of Islam unilaterally accepted all the conditions of the Makkan leaders. However, at the Prophet's suggestion a clause was included in it, specifying that for the next ten years no war would take place between Muslims and the Makkans, directly or indirectly. After the finalization of this document the Prophet left Hudaybiya for Madinah.

The danger of war taking place at any time was thus precluded, and now that peace prevailed, the Prophet set about the strengthening of *dawah* work. One task in this connection entailed the sending of *dawah* letters to the rulers and kings whose kingdoms lay around the borders of Arabia, for instance, to the rulers respectively of Syria and Egypt.

The Prophet's companions were sent to deliver a *dawah* letter to each of these rulers, only one of whom showed any adverse reaction to its receipt, namely, the King of Persia. He considered it beneath his dignity to accept such a letter, so he tore it apart. When the Prophet received this news, he said: "The Emperor of Persia has himself torn his kingdom in pieces."

With this one exception all the kings and rulers showed due respect to the letters sent by the Prophet. Many rulers sent the messengers back with gifts for the Prophet and some of them even accepted Islam, like for instance, Negus the king of Abyssinia.

The Hudaybiya treaty, although apparently in favour of the Makkans, proved of tremendous benefit to Islam. This was so, because when people came to know that a no-war pact had been arrived at between the Quraysh and the Prophet of Islam, an atmosphere of peace prevailed between the two parties. As a result people began moving from place to place without any obstacle in their way. The Makkan and other Arabian tribes began visiting Madinah, while the Madinans began visiting other non-Muslim tribes.

During this free interaction Islam inevitably became a subject of general discussion. Consequently, the call of Islam spread rapidly everywhere. The Arabs, becoming acquainted with the virtues of Islam, began to enter its fold in large numbers. Eventually within a mere two years, the number of Muslims increased enormously.

Now, two years after the signing of this treaty, the

Quraysh of Makkah committed an act of aggression against an ally of the Prophet, and in so doing violated the Hudaybiya treaty. After this incident the Prophet announced that the peace agreement had been repealed. Later, along with ten thousand of his companions, he left for Madinah. It is worth noting that there were only fourteen hundred Muslims to accompany the Prophet on his earlier journey to Hudaybiya, whereas on the present journey his companions numbered ten thousand.

Faced with this strength in numbers, the Makkans found themselves helpless. Therefore they conceded their defeat without any resistance. Makkah was thus conquered in 8 A.H. without any armed encounter.

The Makkan idolaters had formerly put up severe resistance to the Prophet of Islam. They had even planned to kill him. They had contrived to involve him in many battles and had many heinous crimes to their credit. They were the worst types of criminals. Therefore, even if all these people had been put to death, this punishment would have been fully justified. But the Prophet of Islam, thanks to his sublime character, did not take any action against them. He did not even reproach them. He unilaterally declared a general amnesty, saying: "Go, you are all free."

Given those circumstances, this was an extraordinary treatment. The Makkan idolaters were sure that, after the victory of Makkah, they would all be slaughtered on account of their unpardonable crimes. But the Prophet of Islam forgave all of them unconditionally. This exceptional latitude deeply convulsed their consciences. Suddenly brought to their senses, they felt within their heart of hearts that their stance of opposition was in no way justified. After such a display of human greatness, they felt that they ought to enter the religious fold of the Prophet of Islam. And this is exactly what happened. All the insolent Makkans surrendered and joined him in his mission as his companions.

After the victory, the Prophet appointed a governor to represent him in Makkah and then left for Taif, accompanied by ten thousand people. During the journey he reached a place which in those days was called Hunayn. Here the path lay between two hills. The tribe of Hawazin of Taif lived on the upper slopes. They had not yet accepted Islam. The Prophet was quietly going along this path and the Muslims were still between the two hills, when 20,000 archers of the Hawazin, who had concealed themselves in a ravine, all of a sudden started raining their arrows down on them.

The Prophet and his companions were in no way prepared for this sudden attack. In the initial stage, the Muslims were confounded and began to flee. But the Prophet remained steadfast. He called out: "O servants of God, come to me." When the Muslims saw that their leader was standing firm in the face of the enemy, they returned with new determination and bravely fought their foes. Suddenly, the course of the battle changed. Now it was the enemy's turn to take flight. The Prophet and his companions emerged victorious. This incident is known in Islamic history as the battle of Hunayan.

After this victory, six thousand members of the Hawazin tribe were taken prisoner along with booty amounting to 24,000 camels, 40,000 goats and 40,000 ounces of silver. These six thousand prisoners were proven war criminals. According to the prevailing custom, they should all have been put to death. But the Prophet of Islam pardoned them all and set them free without imposing any conditions. This extraordinary treatment gave a severe jolt to their consciences. They had the most profound sense of how wrong their aggressiveness was; having been shown such unusual clemency by Muhammad, the Prophet of Islam, they were honour-bound to enter the fold of the religion brought by him to mankind. And that is precisely what they did. All the people of the Hawazin tribe—both men and women—accepted Islam.

Now the Prophet reached Taif, which was the only fortified town in the Arabian peninsula. At his approach, the townpeople barricaded themselves inside the city. The Prophet and his companions stayed there for three weeks. When there was no sign of their surrendering, the Prophet retreated and left for Madinah.

Makkah enjoyed the central position in ancient Arabia, playing the role of the leader. Now when Makkah was brought into the fold of Islam under the leadership of the Prophet, the entire situation changed. Now the other tribes of Arabia felt that they too should adopt the same religion, i.e. Islam, as had been adopted by the Makkans.

Subsequently, Arabia witnessed the widespread and novel development of far-flung tribes sending their representatives in the form of delegations to Makkah in order that they might enter the fold of Islam, and thus, by entering into a new covenant with the Prophet of Islam, regularize their relations with the Islamic state. That year, delegations of this nature came in such large numbers that it became known as the year of delegations. In this way, one after another, all the tribes of Arabia, including the Taif, entered the fold of Islam.

After having consolidated the power of Islam in Arabia, the Prophet decided to perform the Hajj pilgrimage. This is known in the history of Islam as *Hajj at al-Wida,* the final pilgrimage. In the last year of his life the Prophet left Madinah for Makkah, accompanied by the Madinan Muslims. When the news spread that the Prophet was going to perform the pilgrimage, various tribes living in Arabia also began thronging Makkah.

Therefore, when the Prophet of Islam performed his first as well as his last pilgrimage, he was joined in this historic act of worship by 125,000 Muslims. The teachings he imparted to the people present on the occasion are preserved in the form of his sermon known as the sermon of *Hajj al al-Wida*—an eternal manifesto of Islam. It is as follows:

"*Truly, your lives, your properties and your honour are sacred to you like the sacredness of this day of yours in this month of yours and in this city of yours. Behold! Everything of the Days of Ignorance has been destroyed under my feet and the blood claims of the Days of Ignorance (the pre-Islamic period) have been remitted. The first shedding of blood for which I forbid vengeance to be taken is the murder of Ibn-Rabiyah, son of Haris, and, indeed, all usury of the Days of Ignorance is forbidden, and the first of our usuries that was forbidden was that of Abbas, son of Abdul Muttalib, and that is entirely forbidden. Fear God concerning women, because you have taken them with the trust of God and made their private parts lawful with the word of God. They have got a right over you and you shall clothe them and feed them in a just manner. And I have left among you a thing which, if you adhere to it, you will never be misguided after me, that is, the Book of God. O people, listen to my words and understand them. Nothing of his brother*" *is lawful for a Muslim except what he himself allows."*

"Listen, do not be disbelievers after I have left you, and start killing one another. Listen, Satan has now little hope of misleading his followers to worship something other than God. But he may still achieve his goal by stirring you up against one another. Fear God as regards women, for they depend upon you. They have a right over you, and you have a right over them. If anyone has anything placed in trust with him, he should return it to its owner." Saying this, the Prophet stretched out both his hands and asked his companions. "Have I conveyed the message?" And again he asked, "Have I conveyed the message?" Then he said, "Those who are present should convey my message to those who are absent, for many of them might be better recipients."

The Prophet of Islam died on 12 Rabiul Awwal 10 A.H., after an illness lasting about two weeks. Before his death he said the last prayer in the Masjid-e-Nabawi, and made Abu Bakr the Imam of this prayer.

The importance attached to the Imam in the congregational prayer was a clear indication that Abu Bakr was going to succeed as the Caliph or the leader of the believers after the Prophet.

The Prophet died in the room attached to the Masjid-e-Nabawi. He was buried in the same place and his grave exists there to this day. Later when Abu Bakr and Umar died, they were also buried to the right and left side of the Prophet.

The Prophet in the Qur'an

The Qur'an says of the Prophet of Islam: "Surely you have a sublime character." (68:4) By far the best commentary on this verse has been provided by Aisha, the Prophet's wife. Her words have been recorded in different books of *hadith*. Replying to a question on the character of the Prophet, Aisha, referring to this verse of the Qur'an, said: "His character was the Qur'an."

This shows that the truest picture of the Prophet of Islam is that which has been expressed in the holy scriptures. There is no doubt about it that the books of *hadith* and *seerah* too provide an authentic source of information about the life of the Prophet. But the Qur'an remains the primary source. The picture of the Prophet which tallies with the relevant statements made therein must be regarded as correct. Here I propose to enlarge upon the study of his life in the light of certain Qur'anic verses.

A Seeker of Truth

The Prophet of Islam is thus addressed in chapter 93:

> *"By the light of day, and by the night when it falls, your Lord has not forsaken you, nor does He abhor you. The life to come holds a richer prize for you than this present life. Surely your Lord will give you what will please you. Did he not find you an orphan and give you shelter? Did He not find you wandering and guide you? Did He not find you poor and enrich you? Therefore, neither oppress the orphan, nor drive away the beggar. But proclaim the bounty of your Lord." (1-11).*

The Prophet Muhammad received prophethood at the age of 40. His life prior to prophethood has been thus alluded to in the Qur'an: "Did He not find you wandering?" The explanation of this verse by Islamic scholars has been recorded in the books of *Tafsir* (commentary of the Qur'an). Some of these comments, recorded in *Tafsir Al-Qurtabi,* are as follows: We found you a seeker. We found you a wanderer, we found you a lover of guidance. (*Tafsir Al Qurtabi,* 20-97).

This state, in brief, may be called that of seeking the truth. That is to say, before his being commissioned as a Messenger of God, he was a seeker of Truth, wandering hither and thither in search of it. In those days he used to withdraw to hills and deserts, and stay, engrossed in contemplation, in the privacy of the cave of Hira. All these acts were manifestations of this search for truth welling up in his heart. This phase has been recorded in detail in the books of *Hadith* and *Seerat.*

From this we learn that, as a preliminary to the discovery of truth, the proper course for the individual would be to go in search of it . As we learn from the Qur'an, one who sincerely seeks the truth will definitely receive guidance, just as the Prophet Muhammad did. The difference between the Prophet and the common man is that the former received guidance with prophethood, while the latter will receive only guidance.

The Prophet As a Human Being

The Qur'an describes the Prophet of Islam as a human being like any other. What distinguished him from others was not his being something other than human, but, rather his being a prophet, as well as being a human being. This is illustrated by the following verses from the Qur'an:

> *Am I anything but a human apostle? (17:93)*

> *I am but a mortal like yourselves. It is revealed to me that your God is one God. (18:110)*

> *Their apostles said to them: We are nothing but mortals like you. (14:11)*

This was something natural, and gave credence to the practical example set by the Prophet of Islam for the benefit of all human beings. It is quite clear that his ability to convince rested on his being a human being like all others; on his having feelings of the same nature as other human beings; and on his being made of the same flesh and blood as others. If all these things had not been found in common between the Prophet and other human beings, the command to follow the example of the Prophet would have been rendered impracticable.

The greatness of the Prophet of Islam lay in adopting a superior code of ethics as a human being, so that he should come up to the highest standard of conduct in all matters. Had he been cast in some superhuman mould, his exemplary character could not have served as a model for human beings.

The Prophet – A Test for People

Objections raised by opponents of the Prophet are thus referred to in the Qur'an:

They ask:

> *'Why has no angel been sent down to him?' If We had sent down an angel, their fate would have been sealed and they would have never been reprieved. If We had made him an angel, We would have given him the semblance of a man and would have thus added to their confusion. (6:8-9)*

In chapter 25 the Qur'an records a similar objection raised by doubters:

They also say:

> *'How is it that this Apostle eats and walks about the market-place? Why has no angel been sent down with him to warn us? or (why) has no treasure been given him, no garden to provide his sustenance?' (25:7-8)*

At another place, the Qur'an says:

> *Nothing prevents men from having faith when guidance is revealed to them but the excuse: 'Could God have sent a human being as an apostle?' (17:94)*

Here is an Arabic saying that will help to clarify these verses. That is, things can be understood properly only by their opposites. When we look at it in the light of this principle, two pictures of the Prophet, very different from one another, appear before us. One picture, according to the above verses, is that which was before his contemporaries. The other, the one we have today, has grown tremendously in stature over the fifteen centuries which have elapsed since his coming to the world. In the ancient picture, the Prophet appears to be a common man standing all alone. In vivid contrast, the picture of him that has emerged after 1500 years has become so sublime that modern attempts to describe him, if they are to do him justice, have to include such expressions as "the pride of all existence," "the emperor of both the worlds", "leader of the Universe", "the crown king of Arabia", and so on.

What is the reason for these two starkly different pictures of one and the same personality? It is that a Prophet in his lifetime appears to his contemporaries as a common man. But over the centuries he acquires the status of an established personality and thus attains historical grandeur.

In the first picture, the Prophet has yet to receive acclaim, while in the second, the Prophet is at the zenith of historical grandeur.

The Qur'an tells us that only that faith is acceptable to God which conforms to the example set by the Companions:

> *"If they believe as you have done, they shall be rightly guided; if they do not, they shall surely be in schism. Against them, God is your all-sufficient defender. He is the All-Hearing, the All-Knowing." (2:137)*

The Companions are those believers who were the Prophet's contemporaries. They saw the initial picture of the Prophet when he had not yet acquired an aura of historical grandeur, yet they recognized the greatness in him. At that time the Prophet appeared to be a common man like any other, and not at all like the extraordinary person that he is described as in today's high-flown terms. The first picture of the Prophet is the real one. The rest is the addition of history. The credit of believing in the prophet can be given, in the real sense of the word, only to a person who eliminates the additions of history and recognizes him as he actually was.

The Knowledge of the Unseen

We learn from the Qur'an that God alone has knowledge of the Unseen. As the Qur'an states:

> *"He alone has knowledge of what is hidden:*
> *His secrets He reveals to none." (72:26)*

The Qur'an has repeatedly made it clear that the Prophet of Islam was not given full knowledge of the world unseen. On certain occasions God revealed something of the unseen world in advance to the Prophet through the angel Gabriel, for instance, the result of the Hudaybiya treaty in the form of a 'clear victory' (chapter 48). But he was not given the power to acquire knowledge of the unseen on his own. This is demonstrated by the following verses from the Qur'an:

> *"Had I possessed knowledge of what is hidden,*
> *I would have availed myself of much that is*
> *good." (7:188)*

> *"I do not say to you that I possess God's*
> *treasures and I do not know what is hidden."*
> *(11:31)*

> *"Say: 'God alone has knowledge of what is hidden. Wait if you will: I too am one of those who wait.'" (10:20)*

> *"These are announcements of the unseen which We reveal to you; neither you nor your people knew them." (11:49)*

These and other verses of this nature prove clearly that the Prophet of Islam had not been given knowledge of the unseen. God's law for the Prophet was that he was given only those things essential to the discharging of his responsibilities as a Prophet. As this task did not relate to the metaphysical, he required no knowledge of the unseen.

It was not the Prophet's duty to demonstrate miraculous feats for the sake of establishing his superiority over others, but rather to guide people by means of *dawah* and counselling. This was the real task of the Prophet, and for its performance there was no need to possess any supernatural powers. That is why no Prophet was endowed with such a faculty.

Ease in Difficulty

In chapter 95 of the Qur'an the Prophet is thus addressed:

> *"Have We not lifted up and expanded your heart and relieved you of the burden which weighed down your back? Have We not given*

you high renown? Every hardship is followed
by ease. When you have finished, resume your
toil, and seek your Lord with all fervour."

One particular aspect of the life of the Prophet of Islam comes before us in these verses. That is, the ability to see ease in difficulty was bestowed upon him by God's grace and guidance; he was able, by dint of courage and determination, to turn disadvantageous situations to advantage, and could continue his activities with hope, even in times of great frustration.

Through certain examples God made this matter clear. For instance, the Prophet of Islam underwent great hardship. His experiences broadened his vision, making him more confident. Ironically, his opponents' false propaganda became the means of spreading his message far and wide, etc.

The followers of the Prophet of Islam should also inculcate this same mentality among themselves. They should develop within themselves the capacity to turn minuses into pluses and convert hardship into ease.

The Sustenance of God

Addressing the Prophet of Islam, the Qur'an states:

"Do not strain your eyes towards the worldly
benefits We have bestowed on some of them,
for with these we seek only to try them. Your

Lord's provision is better and more lasting. Enjoin prayer on your people and be diligent in its observance. We demand nothing of you: We shall Ourself provide for you. Blessed shall be the end of the devout." (20:131-132)

The Prophet led his life like other people and in the same world. However, where common men set their sights on collecting more and more worldly goods for themselves, the Prophet did not make this world his goal. He was not desirous of material benefits; rather the world for him became a means of spiritual provision.

We find that in this world those who adopt the life of faith and *dawah* suffer hardship. On the other hand, those who have not devoted themselves to discharging such responsibilities lead their lives amidst material comforts and pleasures. By highlighting this difference between a life of comfort and a life of hardship, i.e. by creating the impression that a worldly life is far better than the godly life, Satan tries to tempt and mislead the believers.

But a deeper examination shows that beyond this apparent difference, there is another dimension, which is far worthier of consideration. It is that worldly possessions are for the purpose of putting human beings to the test, and as such, are of a temporary nature. Those who are preoccupied with material things have nothing in store for their eternal life, while a believer, a *dayee* receives by his association with God something more precious than all the things of the world. That is, remembrance of God, thought of the life hereafter, worship, a life of piety, devotion to God, and concern that the servants of God may be saved from His chastisement. All this is provision as well, but of far higher a quality than material things, and will translate for the *dayee* into endless bliss in the life Hereafter.

Basic Task

Addressing the Prophet in chapter 74 of the Qur'an, God says:

> *"You who are wrapped up in your vestment, arise and give warning. Magnify your Lord, cleanse your garment and keep away from all pollution. Bestow no favours expecting gain. Be patient for your Lord's sake." (74:1-7)*

According to these verses the actual task of the Prophet consists of warning the people of the serious consequences in the life to come, regarding their actions in this world. This duty can be performed only by one whose heart is filled with the greatness of God; who possesses a high moral character; who keeps away from all evil; who does good without any hope of return and who suffers patiently all the hardships inflicted by others.

Four Responsibilities

The Prophet of Islam is said to be the answer to Abraham's prayer. When Abraham settled his son Ismail and his wife Hajira in the deserts of Hijaz, according to the Qur'an he prayed thus:

> *"Send forth to them a messenger of their own people who shall declare to them Your revelations and instruct them in the book and in wisdom and purify them. You are the Mighty, the Wise One." (2:129)*

The first task of the Prophet was to receive God's revelations and communicate them to man, i.e. he had to recite the verses of the Qur'an and explain them to his hearers. Innumerable signs within human nature and in the outside world have been placed there by God so that man may realize Him through them. The second task of the Prophet was, therefore, to reveal these signs, and give man the insight to enable him to experience his Lord.

Insight implies wisdom, so that when man has developed the insight to see God's signs; when he has moulded his mind to the teachings of the Qur'an, a kind of intellectual light begins to shine within him. His cerebral level is raised to a point from which he is able to experience higher realities. In all matters he is able to arrive at the right conclusions as desired by God.

Tazkia means purifying the soul of unfavourable elements in order that a man may, in a favourable atmosphere, elevate himself to the culminating point of spiritual development. Then finally the Prophet strove to prepare people whose souls should be free from all preoccupations except their devotion to God, who should be free also from psychological complexities, so that they might be capable of finding the spiritual sustenance placed by God in the universe for His devoted servants.

These four tasks were the four basic parts of the mission of the Prophet of Islam. All his activities were directed solely to achieving these objectives enumerated above. After the Prophet those who rise to the task of reforming the people have to work along the same lines as were followed by the Prophet on the basis of divine guidance.

Communicating God's Message

The Prophet was thus addressed by God in the Qur'an:

> *Apostle, proclaim what is revealed to you from your Lord; if you do not, you will not have conveyed His message. God will protect you from all men. He does not guide the unbelievers. (5:67)*

This verse shows that, the actual basic task assigned by God to the Prophet was communication of His message. This task had two aspects: firstly, the duty assigned to him as a Messenger of God entailed the performance of the task of communication of the divine message, and secondly, the same task served to protect the Prophet.

Whenever a prophet calls for an uncompromising acceptance of truth, he has to face a severe reaction from his *madu*, or congregation. But this reaction is not shown by the secular people. In most cases it comes from individuals who have established their leadership in the name of religion.

This reaction on the part of those addressed was something natural. For the pure call of the Prophet would amount to discrediting those who already held sway on the basis of self-styled religion. This is a situation which is unavoidable but which the preacher of truth has to face. However, its effect is confined only to the sphere in which the divine law of human trial is operative. It can never happen that opponents become so powerful as to put a stop to the *dawah* campaign altogether, or succeed in preventing this mission from reaching its completion. A true call must reach its target of *dawah* according to the divine plan. Therefore, no power on earth can stop it from remaining unfulfilled. Once the message has been fully communicated, it is for the *madu* to accept or reject it, either fully or in part.

Unilateral Well-Wishing

At the battle of Uhud (3 A.H.) the number of Islam's opponents far exceeded that of the Muslims. Consequently, the latter suffered great losses. Even the Prophet of Islam was injured. Bleeding profusely, the Prophet could not but utter these words: How will those people receive guidance who treat their Prophet in this way, one who calls them towards their Lord. (*Tafsir Ibn Kathir,*1/403).

This was a clear case of grave injustice on the part of the Prophet. And God disapproved of an utterance of this nature. The angel Gabriel was immediately sent by God to the Prophet with these words of caution:

> *It is no concern of yours whether He will forgive or punish them. They are wrongdoers.*
> (3:128)

It was thus incumbent on the Prophet to become his *madu's* well-wisher, even when he was subjected to all kinds of oppression and injustice, to pray for those who cast stones at him, to treat the insolent gently, to show love and affection for those who hated him; to continue to advise his hearers to follow the right path, leaving his own personal fate to God.

This example set by the Prophet has to be adopted, unconditionally, by the *dayee* in his dealings with the *madu*. No other course is lawful for a preacher of truth.

A Positive Response

Addressing the Prophet of Islam, God says in the Qur'an:

> *"Call men to the path of your Lord with wisdom and mild exhortation. Reason with them in the most courteous manner. Your Lord best knows those who stray from His path and best knows those who are rightly guided."* (16:125)

The Qur'an says at another place:

> *And who speaks better than he who calls others to the service of God, does what is right and says: 'I am one of the Muslims.' Good and evil deeds are not alike. Requite evil with good, and he between whom and you is enmity will become your dearest friend. (41:33-34)*

These two verses indicate the missionary character of the Prophet of Islam. The call of *dawah* is good in intention, having nothing in it but mercy for man. However, the demand of *dawah* is that man rectify his own mistakes, that he abandon one life for another. This kind of change is generally very difficult in one's personal life. That is why the *dayees* have to suffer bad treatment at the hands of the *madu*.

If the *dayee* reacts negatively in such situations, the propitious atmosphere between *dayee* and *madu*— an atmosphere which is essential to preserve for the carrying out of the task of *dawah*—will be vitiated. That is why the Prophet was enjoined to return good behaviour for the bad behaviour of the *madu,* i.e. so that the atmosphere of *dawah* should not be disturbed. Finally, the time will come when the message of truth finds its place in the hearts of the people, turning opponents into companions of the Prophet.

The picture that emerges from these verses of the way of the Prophet is one bearing the stamp of his unconditionally good character. The gaze of the Prophet was not fixed on the present state of his hearers, but rather on their future. If anyone treated him badly, he adopted an attitude of restraint, being convinced that, at some future date his addressees would certainly understand the importance of the truth, at which point nothing would stop them from accepting it.

In the eyes of the Prophet the enemy too was a friend; he saw today's opponents as tomorrow's supporters.

The Patient Attitude

In chapter no. 46 of the Qur'an the Prophet is thus addressed by God:

> *Bear up then with patience, as did the steadfast apostles before you, and do not seek to hurry on their doom. On the day when they behold the scourge with which they are threatened, their*

life on earth will seem to them no longer than
an hour. That is but a warning and none but
the evil-doers will be destroyed. (46:35)

The Prophet's most dominant trait was patience. One who calls for truth has to resist any tendency to impetuousness, which means unconditionally refraining from persecution of the *madu*. Despite the *madu's* denial and stubbornness, he continues peacefully and amicably to convey to them the message of Truth.

The *dayee* has to be the *madu's* well-wisher in all circumstances, howsoever unpleasant the experiences he may be undergoing. This unbounded patience is essential, for without it the communication of the divine message can never be fully undertaken.

All the prophets of God, in all ages, have performed the task of proclaiming the truth with total patience and perseverance. In future, those who, following in the footsteps of the Prophet work for the communication of the truth on his behalf, shall also have to adopt the same pattern. Only one who has the courage to bear all the difficulties created by the *madu* will be recognized as a *dayee* by God.

Rising Above the Psychology of Reaction

The Qur'an, addressing mankind at large, says:

"There has now come to you an apostle of your
own, one who grieves at your sinfulness and

cares for you; one who is compassionate and merciful to true believers." Then, addressing the Prophet, it says: If they give no heed, say: 'God is all sufficient for me. There is no god but Him. In Him I have put my trust. He is the Lord of the Glorious Throne.'" (9:128-129)

In these verses, the Prophet emerges in his struggle for Islam as one having full confidence in God the Almighty. The key to all treasure lies with Him. The Prophet stands on the firm ground of this same faith and conviction. It is therefore but natural that his entire faith should rest on one God alone and that he should devote himself to the service of Truth, free from all fears or the pressures of expediency.

We are told in this verse that the messenger of God was extremely kind and compassionate towards people. He was so pained to see others in trouble that it was as though he himself were in distress. He was extremely keen to bring guidance to people. What inspired him to engage himself in this struggle to proclaim the truth was the feeling of wishing others well, and was certainly unrelated to the fulfillment of any personal or communal goal. He rose for the betterment of the people and not to satisfy his own personal interests.

According to Abdullah ibn Masood, the Prophet observed: People are falling in the fire like flies and I hold them by the waist to prevent them from falling into the fire. (*Musnad Ahmad*)

The picture this hadith gives us of the Prophet defines for all time what a *dayee* of Islam should be like. He should have two special qualities in particular: First, he should have complete trust in God; second, his heart should have nothing but love and well-wishing for the *madu*. He will certainly face all sorts of complaints and animosity from the *madu*; there might be friction and discord, communal as well as material, between the *dayee* and the *madu*. But, despite all this, he has to adopt a non-confrontational policy in all matters of contention, never allowing any other feeling for the *madu* to enter his heart, save that of love and well-wishing.

A *dayee* has to rise above the psychology of reaction. He has to become a unilateral well-wisher of the *madu*, howsoever adverse the attitude adopted by the latter.

The Personality of the Prophet of Islam

God himself was the patron of the Prophet of Islam. One piece of guidance He gave to him on different occasions was the cultivation of positive thinking. In this world everyone is faced with unpleasant incidents. And the Prophet of Islam had his share of unpleasantness. On all such occasions God showed him how there may be a favourable aspect to seemingly unfavourable happenings.

In ancient Makkah when the Prophet of Islam began to spread the call of monotheism, he was faced with severe difficulties. At that time he was advised in the Qur'an not to become upset in the face of adversity, for, in this world, every hardship was accompanied by ease. For example, his opponents started issuing false propaganda on a large scale regarding his activities, and made all kinds of allegations against him. At that time God advised him that through this propaganda his message was being conveyed to broad sections of society. Therefore, the Prophet should not take it as damaging to his efforts, but should regard it rather as a means of introducing his mission to the public.

Despite the propagation of his message for about twenty years, the Prophet and his companions still remained in a minority in Arabia, the idolaters being in the majority. At that time the Prophet and his companions were reminded by God of how many times, by His grace, it had happened that a small group had prevailed over a larger group (2:249).

Then in 3 A.H., the Battle of Uhud took place, in which the Muslims were defeated by the idolaters—an apparently discouraging event. But even on that occasion God again pointed out only the bright and positive aspect of the matter:

> *"If you sustained an injury at the battle of Uhud, they, the enemy, also sustained injuries at the battle of Badr, and We alternate these vicissitudes among mankind."* (3:140)

On a parallel with this was the signing of the Hudaybiyya peace treaty, which took place in 6 A.H., between the Prophet of Islam and the idolaters. This peace treaty ostensibly signalled the political defeat of the Muslims. But when this event was commented upon in the Qur'an, God said, on the contrary, that He had given them a 'clear victory' over their adversaries (48:1).

This meant that despite their apparent political defeat, the Muslims had achieved a moral victory, which would in the end result in total victory, etc.

This divine training made the Prophet of Islam into an individual who was free from all negative thoughts. He may without doubt be called the greatest positive thinker of the world.

Trust in God

During the journey of emigration when the Prophet of Islam left Makkah for Madinah, he was accompanied only by Abu Bakr Siddiq. This was a journey full of risks. The Makkans, thirsting for his blood, would certainly pursue him, therefore the Prophet took every possible precaution. Although he had to go to Makkah, he went in the opposite direction, and reached the cave of Thaur, where he stayed with Abu Bakr for a few days.

When the news of his emigration reached the Makkan leaders, they sent their people out in all directions in order to catch and kill him before his arrival at Madinah. When the Prophet and Abu Bakr Siddiq were hiding in the cave, a search party came so close that they were clearly visible from inside. Abu Bakr Siddiq, watching them standing at the entrance of the cave with their drawn swords, said to the Prophet that if any one of them looked at his feet, he would find them. The Prophet replied with total confidence:

> *O Abu Bakr, what do you think of those two who have God as the third companion?* (Seerah *ibn Kathir, 2:243*)

These words uttered by the Prophet of Islam were of such towering significance that they have perhaps no precedent in the entire history of the human species. Even at that moment in time, when he was undoubtedly in the most perilous situation, his trust in God was so great that even the mightiest tempest could not have shaken it. At that juncture it was this limitless confidence that inspired the utterance of such bold words.

The Prophet's State of Mind During Worship

The Prophet of Islam worshipped God daily, during the day as well as at night. There is a tradition which tells us the state of his heart at the time of worship. Ali narrates that when the Prophet said his prayers, these were the words of invocation that often came to his lips at the time of bowing down:

> *O God, I bow before You, I believe in You and I have surrendered myself to you. My ears, my eyes, my brain, my bones, my nerves have all submitted to You.*

Ali has further recorded that when the Prophet of Islam used to place his forehead on the ground at the time of prostration, these words would come to his lips:

> God, I have prostrated myself before You, I have believed in You, I have surrendered myself to You. My face has bowed to the one who has created it, gave it shape, made ears and eyes. God is most Blessed, the best Creator. (Sahih Muslim)

These traditions tell us of the feelings of the Prophet when he was engaged in worship. He used to be totally immersed in God's glory and majesty. The sense of God's greatness and his own humility in comparison were so overwhelming that they created a tempest within his heart. His worship was akin to a tangible presence before God the Almighty. His worship had a highly intense, living quality to it, and was not just a set of rituals.

Great Concern over Giving Guidance

The Prophet was thus addressed in the Qur'an:

> "These are verses of the clear Book. You will perhaps fret yourself to death on account of their unbelief. If We will, We can reveal to them a sign from heaven before which they will bow their heads in utter humility. (26:1-4)

This and other such pieces of evidence tell us how eager the Prophet was to give guidance to his people. The expression, 'You will perhaps fret yourself to death,' shows the degree of well-wishing which the Prophet had for his *madu*. The *dawah* act in the true sense is an outcome of the pure feeling of benevolence towards others. The Prophet of Islam communicated the call of truth to his people with this absolute feeling of magnanimity. He struggled to the utmost to keep to this path. Despite this, the majority refused to accept his message. And the Prophet began to worry so deeply about their guidance that he would spend days and nights in a state of extreme restlessness.

Here, in this verse, the statement, "Perhaps you will fret yourself to death" does not mean that he should stop communicating the message. Rather, these words testify to the fact that the Prophet had discharged his responsibilities as a Prophet to the greatest possible degree. His concern for others' guidance causing him such great distress is the most important attribute of his personality. Without doubt he had reached the ultimate in this matter, i.e. in the communication of God's message.

According to a tradition, the Prophet of Islam once observed: "My Lord offered to turn the valley of Makkah into one of gold. I said, 'No, my Lord. Instead I want that one day I should have my fill and the next day go hungry. And when I am hungry, I should beseech You and remember You, and when I have my fill, praise You and thank You.'"

Muhammad was the Prophet of Islam but, according to the Qur'an, he was also a human being. Therefore, he took care to experience all such circumstances as would produce divine or spiritual feelings, for feelings are very much conditioned by one's circumstances in life. For this reason he did not opt to remain forever in a state of comfort and happiness. On the contrary, he made it a point to face difficult situations as well, in order that feelings of helplessness might be produced within him. Similarly, he also desired good situations for himself, so that these might produce feelings of thanksgiving and a desire to praise God.

Courage and Fearlessness

The battle of Hunain at which the Prophet of Islam was present, took place in 8 A.H. His engagement in the battle was, as it happened, quite fortuitous. It seems, that when the Prophet was travelling with his companions, all of a sudden the tribe of Hawazin, without provocation, rained down arrows on the Muslims. The Muslims could not stand up to this unexpected attack. Most of them began running off. But the Prophet and some of his companions stood their ground firmly and fearlessly. With arrows raining down on them from all sides, the Prophet, remained sitting on his donkey, and recited this couplet: I am a Prophet and I do not lie. I am the son of Abdul Muttalib. (*Biography of the Prophet* by Ibn Kathir, Vol 3/623)

This incident shows that the Prophet of Islam possessed the highest degree of courage. His heart was completely free from all fear. Not even the hail of arrows could make his steps falter. The conviction of his being in possession of the truth, and that he was on the right path, had made him totally invincible. He once observed: "I see what you do not see. I hear what you do not hear. The sky is crackling and it is liable to do so. By God, there is no space, not even an inch where an angel has not bowed his head in submission to God. By God, if you knew what I know, you would cry more and laugh less. Women would cease to give you any pleasure. Calling God, you would have left for the woods and the jungles." The narrator of this tradition, Abu Dhar Ghafari says (so that he should be spared facing the Day of Judgement): "I wish I were a tree cut off by its roots." (*Mishkat al Masabih,* 3/169)

Although these observations have been addressed to others, they, in fact, describe the psychological condition of the Prophet of Islam himself. This shows how his days and nights were spent, what his feelings were, what his thinking was and what the greatest news was that he had to communicate to others with the greatest urgency.

We find from the Qur'an that God had entrusted

the Prophet of Islam with the mission to tell human beings of the reality of life, and warn them of the horrors of Doomsday. The world could not be a place of happiness and comfort for one upon whom such a responsibility had devolved. One so placed could not enjoy the things that made the ignorant happy. Such traditions have therefore been recorded in the books of *Hadith* to the effect that the Prophet used to remain in perpetual anguish.

At the age of 25, the Prophet of Islam married a virtuous Arab lady called Khadijah. He had a happy married life with her until he received the prophethood at the age of 40. When he came home after the first revelation, his wife spread his bed for him and asked him to take some rest. The Prophet replied: 'O, Khadijah, Where is comfort?' (The days of comfort are gone.)

Sense of Equality

Abdullah ibn Masood, a companion of the Prophet, narrates that on the occasion of the battle of Badr, when they set forth, they did not have enough mounts. There was one camel for three of them, so they mounted by turns. Ali ibn Abi Talib, Abu Lubaba and the Prophet shared one camel. When the two companions had to take their turns, they would both ask the Prophet to mount instead of them, saying that they would continue on foot. The Prophet would reply, "You are not stronger than me in walking, and I am not less in need of God's reward than you." (*Musnad* Ahmad, 1/422)

This incident reveals the kind of feelings which dominated the Prophet when he was amongst his people. In spite of being a prophet, he regarded himself as a human being like any other. He felt that he needed the divine reward like the rest of humanity and had to earn it just as others did. He was free of all feelings of pride and had no superiority complex whatsoever. Everything he felt for others came from the depths of his heart.

One who has achieved the realization of God in the true sense of the word becomes somewhat similar in his mental state. Man is totally cut to size after this experience. The certainty of the unfathomable grandeur of the Almighty divests one of all feelings of one's own greatness. The feeling of smallness as compared to the greatness of God so dominated the Prophet that, despite being a great man, he was unable to think of himself as being in any way extraordinary.

The deep realization of God the Almighty rids one of all feelings of personal grandeur. One regards oneself only as His servant, and nothing more.

The Prophet's sentiments were marked by absolute perfection. No less perfect was his willingness to serve his Creator.

Concern about the Hereafter

We learn from a tradition that once when the Prophet of Islam was at home with his wife Umm Salmah, he sent her maidservant on an errand of some urgency. She took some time to come back. So Umm Salmah went to the window and saw that the maid was watching some children playing a game in the street. When she eventually came back, signs of anger appeared on the Prophet's face. At that time the Prophet had a *miswak* (a small twig used as a toothbrush) in his hand.

"If it wasn't for the fear of retribution on the Day of Judgement, I would have hit you with this *miswak*," said the Prophet to the maid.

The Prophet of Islam warned the people of the chastisement of Doomsday. This incident shows that this warning was not just meant for others. He too always went in fear of it. He wanted people to live in this world in such a way that the fear of God's chastisement should be embedded in their hearts. The same applied to the Prophet himself. The impending Doomsday was a matter of grave concern to everyone including himself. His prophethood did not in any sense exempt him from accountability in the life Hereafter. (That is, he did not feel that he was above accountability.)

Respect for Human Beings

In ancient Madinah some Jewish tribes were settled alongside the Muslims. One day the Prophet of Islam was visiting a part of Madinah, where there was a funeral procession passing by. The Prophet was seated at that time, but on seeing the funeral procession, he stood up in deference to the deceased. Some companions who were with the Prophet at the time, said: "O Prophet, it was the funeral of a Jew." On hearing this, the Prophet replied: "Was he not a human being?" (*Sahih Al-Bukhari, Kitab al-Janaiz*)

We may judge from the Prophet's behaviour on this occasion what kind of feelings he had in his heart for other human beings. He considered everyone as a human being. Everyone appeared to him worthy of respect, to whatever nation or community he might belong. Everyone was equally a creature of God. Everyone served to remind him of God as a perfect Creator. That is why his heart was filled with feelings of love and respect for all human beings. Hatred was totally against his nature.

Humanitarian Feeling

It has been recorded in *Sahih* al-Bukhari and *Sahih* Muslim, how once, when the Prophet had borrowed some money from a merchant in Madinah, the latter came to him to demand the repayment of his debt. He was rude and bitter in his manner. He even went to the extent of saying that all those belonging to the family of Abdul Muttalib (the Prophet's grandfather) kept deferring payment of their debts.

The Companions became angry on hearing such harsh, uncalled for words from him, and wanted to beat him. But the Prophet stopped them from doing so. He said: "Leave him alone. For a creditor has a right to demand payment, even though he may be harsh in doing so."

This incident tells us of the feelings of the Prophet in controversial matters: he did not think only in terms of his own self, but was ever willing to make full concessions to the other party. No doubt, the merchant's manner of speaking was contrary to all the norms of decent behaviour. He attacked the Prophet's honour and prestige, saying things which were sure to provoke his people. But the Prophet, owing to his high sense of justice, ignored all the unpleasantness. Instead of giving in to his own feelings, he made concessions to the feelings of the other party. Overlooking all the insulting aspects of the matter, he thought only of the right of the creditor to demand repayment of his debt.

Trust in Realities

In 6 A.H., after lengthy negotiations, a treaty was arrived at between the Prophet of Islam and the idolators. When the articles of the treaty were finalized, the Prophet started dictating them. Ali ibn Abi Talib began committing them to paper, but when the Prophet dictated these words: "The following is the text of a pact reached by Muhammad, the Prophet of God and Suhayl ibn Amr," Suhayl, the non-Muslim delegate of the Quraysh, took offence at this. He said: "The source of contention or the cause of hostility between us is due to the very fact that we do not believe that you are a prophet of God. If we accepted you as a prophet, then all opposition would cease on its own." He then asked the Prophet to dictate instead: "This is a pact reached by Muhammad ibn Abdullah."

Ali said that he could not erase the words "Muhammad the Prophet of God." So the Prophet himself deleted those words and then asked Ali to write instead "Muhammad, son of Abdullah."

The real status of the Prophet of Islam was that he was the Prophet of God: his entire mission rested on this claim. Erasing the words 'Messenger of God' was like erasing one's own actual identity, which was a very delicate matter. It amounted to giving the impression that he himself was in doubt of his own identity. That is why Umar Faruq, in a state of great agitation, came to Abu Bakr and said: "Is he not the Prophet of God?" (p. 320)

Yet the Prophet of Islam did not attach importance to any of these things, the reason being that he had risen so high that he was able to penetrate the veils of appearances; he lived in the sphere of realities. And it was thanks to this psychology that he could feel that, irrespective of the words written on paper, what would ultimately prevail would be the Truth.

The Prophet's unshakable conviction that he was God's Prophet was enough for him not to attach importance to an error which would surely be rectified by the sheer weight of realities. Defense and support of his position would eventually become immaterial.

An Uncompromising Attitude

As recorded in the traditions, some companions of the Prophet, on seeing signs of premature ageing in the Prophet, asked him: "O Prophet of God, what has aged you so soon?" The Prophet replied: "It is chapters (of the Qur'an) like *Hud* that has aged me." (*Tafsir ibn Kathir*, 2/435)

What is there in particular in the chapter *Hud* which had such an extraordinary effect on him that he began to look old? Verse 113 gives us some idea: It says, "And do not incline towards those who do wrong, lest the fire touch you. And you shall have no friends besides Allah, nor shall you be helped." (11:113)

This verse pertains to the time when the Prophet of Islam had communicated his message of *dawah* openly, but had found the majority of the people unwilling to accept it. The chiefs and the leaders in particular were adamant in their denial of the message. At such a juncture the *dayee* feels that to bring the *madu* closer to accepting the message, some changes in the basic message of *dawah* might be made in order to make it acceptable. That is why the Prophet is adjured not to "incline toward those who do wrong," i.e., the Prophet of Islam was strictly forbidden to show any kind of leniency towards the unbelievers, because what God desired more than anything else in the matter of *dawah* was the pure and simple proclamation of the truth. Now, this cannot be done where inclinations are yielded to or compromises are made. This is what made the Prophet of Islam old before his time. The truth is that in the present world the communication of the truth, based on compromises is the easiest, and ensures the popularity of the *dayee*, while the unadulterated communication of the truth is the most difficult task, making the preacher seem undesirable to others. If the former goes by smooth and even paths, the latter goes by stony paths strewn with thorns.

The Prophet knew that the proclamation of truth could only be that which is pure, without any human interpolation or addition. It was the seriousness of this matter that affected the Prophet so greatly and caused him to age prematurely.

Despite Victory

Makkah was the birthplace of the Prophet of Islam. Yet the Makkans compelled him to leave what was his own home town. That was the beginning of a bitter 20 year phase of oppression and violence. However, circumstances ultimately changed for the better, and in 8 A.H. Makkah was conquered. He now returned victoriously to the very city which, as a victim of oppression, he had been compelled to leave.

But the state of his heart at that time was totally different from what we find in conquerors in general. Eyewitnesses relate that, at the time of his entry on camel back into Makkah, he was a complete picture of modesty. The extraordinary divine succour he had received made his head bow so low that his beard was touching the camel's saddle. (*Seerah* ibn Hisham, 4/24)

We learn from traditions that, after entering Makkah, he stood at the gate of the Kabah and said: "There is no god but the one God. He has no partner. He fulfilled His promise, helped His servant and defeated His opponents all alone." (*Seerah* ibn Hisham, p. 33)

Victory is an occasion for joyous celebration, for displaying pride, etc. But such activities are indulged in only by those whose eyes are on their own selves; who regard victory as their own achievement. But the psychology of the Prophet of Islam was totally different. For him the victory was only apparently his own achievement. For him it was God alone who was the author of his success.

A Prayer

Many prayers of the Prophet of Islam, recorded in the books of *Hadith*, tell us of his inner personality. They tell us the kind of tumultuous feelings which constantly convulsed his heart and mind, and what kinds of feelings and thoughts found a place in his inner self.

One of the prayers that often came to his lips was: My God, show me the truth in the form of the truth and grant that we may adhere to it, and O my God, show me falsehood in the form of falsehood and grant me protection from it, and O God, show us things as they are.

In the present world a veil of doubts is cast over realities. One who knows things only by their appearances can never understand their innate value. The Prophet was moved at this. He spontaneously called upon God to ask Him to grant him the blessing of being able to see the reality, so that he might understand things exactly as they were; so that he might form right opinions which corresponded exactly with the true state of affairs. True realization is not possible without right thinking. Similarly right actions cannot emanate from wrong thinking. It was feelings such as these which, because of their intensity, gave this prayer its unique form. This prayer is, in effect, a picture of the believing heart possessed in the most sublime form by the Prophet.

Prophetic Wisdom

One of the qualities of the Prophet of Islam was his great vision, as a result of which he urged his followers to adopt a wise approach in all their dealings. A number of sayings on this subject have appeared in books of *Hadith*. For instance he observed:

We must not feel envy except for two kinds of people: those who, when given wealth, spend generously in the path of Truth, and those who, when given wisdom, judge accordingly and shed its light upon others.

Abdullah ibn Abbas said that the Prophet of Islam embraced him and prayed to God to grant him wisdom. (*Fathul Bari*, 7/126)

A large number of traditions have been recorded which underscore the importance of wisdom. For instance, the Prophet of Islam said: How good is the gathering at which wise sayings are uttered. Similarly, he said: There is no better gift than words of wisdom. (*Ad Darmi*)

The importance of wisdom is so great that we are urged not to hesitate in accepting any words of wisdom, even from other nations or communities. The Prophet once observed: "A piece of wisdom is a believer's own lost possession, so wherever he finds it, he should adopt it as if he is the most deserving of it."

In some traditions wisdom and deeper understanding have even more importance attached to them than worship. As recorded by Al-Tirmidhi and Ibn Majah, "one learned religious scholar carries more weight than one thousand worshippers."

The Prophet's entire life was filled with examples of wisdom. While discharging his responsibilities, he adopted the way of wisdom on all occasions and at all stages. Here are some examples from his life:

On the Occasion of Confrontations

When the Prophet was thirty five years old, before the time of his prophethood, a situation arose in Makkah, which called for tactful handling. The walls of the Kabah, which had collapsed for some reason, were being rebuilt by the Quraysh tribe, and in the process a problem arose as to who should be given the privilege of laying the black stone in its place in the Kabah wall. Since it was a matter of great prestige, everyone wanted this honour for himself.

The dispute on this question continued for several

days without there being any amicable solution in sight. Finally, all the tribesmen concerned showed their willingness to accept a suggestion made by one of their senior members, viz., that the person who entered the Kabah the earliest the following morning would be appointed as their arbitrator. The next morning when they all saw that the first person to enter the Kabah was the Prophet, they all chorused: "He is the trustworthy one (Al-Ameen). We shall all abide by his decision."

The Prophet then asked the people to bring a sheet of cloth. When it was produced, he spread it on the ground and placed the black stone on it. Then he asked the people to hold the sheet by the edges and carry it to the wall of the Kabah. The Prophet then placed the black stone in the wall with his own hands.

This act of the Prophet serves as a fine example of how a controversial matter can be amicably solved, and to everyone's entire satisfaction, by having everyone participate. Such matters often turn into prestige issues. But if the matter is wisely handled and people are assured that they will not lose face, no difficulty will be faced in addressing the problem.

The Starting Point

When the Prophet of Islam received prophethood in Makkah, he opted for a particular line of action in the spreading of his message. He used to go to the people and tell them: "Say there is no God but the one God and you will be saved." That is, abandon idolatry and worship only one God and you will earn salvation.

This shows the correct prophetic method of Islamic *dawah* (or Islamic movement). That is, first of all, to bring about a change in the character and thinking of the people through peaceful intellectual campaigns. Only when this initial work has been performed to a considerable extent should practical steps be taken and only if circumstances permit.

Tolerating Insult

Ibn Ishaq, the Prophet's earliest biographer, says that the Quraysh had given the Prophet the nomenclature of *Mudhammam* (the condemned one), then they used to heap abuses on him using this derogatory name. The Prophet said to his companions, "Don't you wonder how God has saved me from the abuses of the Quraysh? They abuse and condemn a person named *Mudhammam,* while I am Muhammad.

During the Makkan period when the Quraysh developed enmity and hatred for the Prophet, they did not like calling him by his actual name, which was Muhammad, because it meant 'praiseworthy.' Therefore, to satisfy their inimical feelings, they named him *Mudhammam,* meaning condemned. So when the Quraysh abused and condemned him, they did not use the word Muhammad, but heaped abuses on one called *Mudhammam.* Even Abu Lahab's wife

Umm Jamil herself came to the prophet and said: You are *Mudhammam* and we reject you (p. 379)

This was undoubtedly an act of great provocation and calculated to cause humiliation. But the Prophet of Islam gave a simple, positive reply. He said that since they abused one they called *Mudhammam,* their abuses did not fall on him, as his name was Muhammad, not *Mudhammam.*

When the Prophet of Islam came to Madinah after migration, Abdullah ibn Ubayy, a tribal chief, turned a dire opponent of the Prophet. He had accepted Islam, but out of jealousy he became his enemy. Defaming, disparaging and slandering the Prophet became his pastime. He was also responsible for the false propaganda against him. It would not be wrong to say that he was his greatest abuser (*shaatim*). Umar Faruq asked for the Prophet's permission to slay him, but the Prophet said; "Leave him alone, otherwise people will start saying that Muhammad kills his own people." (*Fathul Bari,* 8/520)

This incident tells us of an important example set by the Prophet, that is to bear humiliation, for if we failed to do so, greater evil would follow and that would result in discrediting God's religion.

No Premature Action

After he received prophethoc d, the Prophet of Islam lived for thirteen years in Makkah where the majority of the Makkans opposed him, tormenting him in every possible way. Owing to his *dawah* struggle, however, about two hundred men and women accepted Islam. These Muslims would say to the Prophet again and again that they wanted to engage in *jihad* against this oppression. But the Prophet always exhorted them to exercise patience. For instance, when Umar Farooq asked for the Prophet's permission to wage *jihad* against the oppression of the Quraysh, the latter replied: O Umar, we are small in number. (*Seerat* Ibn Kathir, 1/441)

During the last days in Makkah about two hundred people in Madinah embraced Islam. When these people learned that the Prophet and his companions were being targeted for oppression, they too asked for the Prophet's permission to wage war against the oppressors, but the Prophet gave them the same reply:

> "Show patience, for I have not been given permission to do battle."

Despite being subjected to all kinds of injustice and oppression for a period of fifteen years, the Prophet unilaterally adopted the path of patience and tolerance. Then for the first time, on the occasion of the battle of Badr, the Prophet went out along with his companions to encounter the enemy. He took this step only when he had received God's clear promise that He would send His angels to the aid of His Messenger. (8:9)

The way of the Prophet of Islam was not to retaliate immediately against any act of oppression. He felt that, despite injustice and oppression on the part of the enemy, the way of patience and avoidance of clashes should be adopted. Practical steps were to be taken only when it was certain that they would yield the desired result.

Avoiding Confrontation

During the thirteen years' period in Makkah, the majority continued to oppose the Prophet, while only a small number of people supported him. When the Makkans found that mere opposition was not enough to extirpate his mission from Makkah, they resolved to remove him from their path by killing him. They unanimously decided that all the leaders of Makkah should attack him together and thus put an end to the movement of monotheism forever.

This was a very precarious situation. One option, which appeared to be the only one, was for the Prophet, along with his companions, to meet the enemy on the battlefield. But the Prophet saw this matter from the point of view of the resultant effect. Since in those circumstances armed confrontation was not going to yield the desired result, the Prophet followed the principle of avoidance and migrated to Madinah from Makkah.

The way of the Prophet of Islam was not to follow a collision course at a time of strife or controversy, but to move away from the point of conflict. Such a course enables one to conserve one's energies in order to utilize them more fruitfully at a later stage.

Concession to Others

An enduring principle of Islam is that which is called 'softening of the heart.' It means to unite people by attempting to produce a soft corner in their hearts. This end can be achieved only by making concessions to others, giving due respect to their sentiments and not harming their interests. This policy of sympathising with others is an important part of Islamic *dawah*. It is to be desired at all times in all human societies.

The Prophet of Islam followed this rule throughout his life. For instance, when he came to Madinah after emigration, many families of Jews and idolaters settled there along with the believers. On reaching there the Prophet issued a statement known as the covenant of Madinah. In this the Prophet declared that each group would enjoy the freedom of their culture and religion; that the controversial matters of all tribes would be settled according to their respective tribal traditions; and that no coercion would be resorted to in matters of religion and culture.

The Prophet made special concessions to the Jews. He even went to the extent of fasting on the days when the Jews fasted until it was held obligatory by a revelation to fast in the month of Ramazan.

Moreover, the Prophet prayed in the direction of Jerusalem, the direction followed by the Jews, for a period of seventeen months, until God's command came to change the orientation towards the Kabah. By doing so, the Prophet aimed at fraternizing with the Jews, in order that they might be brought closer to his faith. (*Tafsir* al-Qurtubi, 2/150)

The way of the Prophet was not to return opposition for opposition. It was rather to make allowances in the face of opposition. His thinking was not to bring people into his fold by means of suppression. On the contrary, his way was to soften their hearts and bring them to his side through affection and kindness.

Secrecy

We read in the annals of history that, prior to the conquest of Makkah, the Prophet gave instructions to his companions to ready themselves for a journey. The Muslims then engaged themselves in the necessary tasks. At that time Abu Bakr came to his daughter, Aisha, wife of the Prophet. She too was busy making preparations for a journey. Abu Bakr asked her: "Has the Prophet ordered you to do so?" Aisha replied in the affirmative. Then Abu Bakr asked her about the destination of this proposed journey. Aisha replied, "By God, I don't know." (*Seerah* ibn Hisham, 3/14)

One of the *sunnah* of the Prophet of Islam was

that, in delicate matters, he always observed strict secrecy. And this is what he did during the campaign of the conquest of Makkah. He left Madinah for Makkah along with ten thousand of his companions, without confiding in them where he was heading. The companions are on record as saying that it was only when they reached the point from where the path led directly to Makkah, that they the realized what their ultimate destination would be.

In matters of strategy, the observance of secrecy is of the utmost importance. Success, in most cases, depends on the fact that the rival party remains completely unaware of one's plans in advance. The Prophet of Islam showed this wisdom all his life.

Accepting the Status Quo

Whenever a controversy arises between two people or two groups, a practical working arrangement ultimately becomes established. An attempt to change this status quo in most cases results in futility or in all-out strife. What normally happens is that the status quo continues. If not, mutual retaliation results in further losses. In this pointless engagement, precious opportunities are also wasted.

In such a controversial matter, the Prophet's *sunnah* is to accept the status quo. The great benefit of this status-quoism is that it gives one the respite to consolidate one's energies. By removing oneself from the scene of controversy, one may strengthen oneself so greatly that a time will come when ultimately the balance of power will change without any major confrontation.

The Prophet of Islam adopted this wise course on the occasion of the drawing up of the Treaty of Hudaybiya. When the Makkans heard that their opponents had gathered at Hudaybiya, they too reached there to stop the Muslims from going any further. The Prophet at this juncture was on his way to Makkah to perform the rite of *Umra* (minor pilgrimage). Thus a situation of deadlock came to be created at Hudaybiya. The Prophet did not resort to breaking this deadlock in order to move ahead. Instead he withdrew and came back to Madinah.

It amounted to accepting the status quo already established between the Prophet and the other party. This wisdom gave the Prophet an opportunity for further consolidation, which became a reality within a period of a mere two years. It was at that stage that the Prophet's victorious entry into Makkah became a possibility.

Ease in difficulty

The Prophet of Islam conquered Makkah in 8 A.H. Then he set off from Makkah for *Taif,* along with his companions. In those days there were no well-laid roads in and around Makkah, and on the journey they had to walk along a narrow path which lay between two hills.

When the Prophet of Islam reached that point, he asked his companions what its name was. They replied that it was called *Azzaiqa*, meaning the "narrow path." The Prophet said:

"No it is rather a broad path." (Seerah *ibn Hisham*, 4/127)

On this journey the Prophet was accompanied by ten thousand of his companions. If they had attempted to go along this path walking several abreast, it would certainly have been difficult to do so, due to its narrowness. But because they went along it in single file, despite its being narrow, it was easy to do so. It was this practical wisdom which the Prophet pointed to in his reply. We find an important secret of life in this incident: the necessity to adapt our strategy to the circumstances. This practice relates to all matters in life. By our being adaptable, all life's difficulties may be resolved.

Strategic Retreat

During the life of the Prophet, in 8 A.H. the battle of Muta took place on the border of Syria, which at that time was under Byzantine rule. The Muslim army, totalling only three thousand, was greatly outnumbered by the enemy forces. Many commanders from the Muslim side fell in the battle. In the last stage Khalid bin Walid, having great military experience, reorganized the Muslim ranks in such a way as to give the impression that massive reinforcements from Madinah had arrived to join the battle. Awed at this, the Romans decided to abandon the battlefield. Finding it pointless to continue the battle, Khalid decided to withdraw, on the principle of tactical retreat, and left for Madinah.

The brave Arabs, always ready to fight to the finish, saw the retreat as a dishonour to them. They failed to understand the wisdom of tactical retreat, and accused the Muslims of fleeing in the face of the enemy. They called them *O Furrar,* that is, those who take flight. When the Prophet heard this, he corrected this wrong impression by telling them that those people had not fled, but had simply withdrawn in order to advance again at some future date, God willing. (*Seerat* ibn Hisham, 3/438)

This saying of the Prophet teaches us that the right step is that which is result-oriented. Fighting to die for honour and prestige is not a desirable act in Islam. If the enemy's numbers are so great as to turn the tide of battle in their favour, hostilities should not be engaged in. Even if a confrontation does take place, tactical retreat should be resorted to, so that preparations may be made for taking the next result-oriented steps.

The Policy of Gradualness in Reform

Aisha, the Prophet's wife, has been recorded as saying that "the first chapters of the Qur'an to be revealed, those making mention of heaven and hell, were short ones. It was only when people became conditioned to accept Islamic teachings, that verses dealing with what is lawful and unlawful began to be revealed. And if injunctions like: 'Do not drink wine,' and 'Do not commit adultery,' had been revealed first, people would have refused to abandon these practices." (Fathul Bari, 8/655)

This tradition tells us of a very important policy of the Prophet. It is the same practical wisdom which is called gradualness. The reform of human beings is a very difficult and complex task. Generally because they have become accustomed to certain ideas and habits, they hold them to be right and proper. That is why they do not readily accept anything new. In such a situation the only way to reform people is to follow the path of wisdom and do everything gradually.

The Prophet of Islam first of all changed the thinking of the people in Arabia. And only when they had developed the ability to accept reforms, did he introduce the commands of the *shariah* to them. If the Prophet had attempted to impose the laws of *shariah* upon them without striving for their intellectual purification—this being against human nature—his efforts towards revolution in Arab society could never have been crowned with success.

Making Concessions as the Situation Requires

In Dhil Hijjah 9 A.H., the Prophet of Islam performed the Hajj which is generally known as the Farewell Pilgrimage. More than one hundred thousand Muslims had gathered to perform the Hajj with the Prophet. Of the many observations made by the Prophet in his sermon, there was one very significant one which amounts to a declaration of human equality. On this occasion the Prophet uttered these historic words: that no Arab had any superiority over a non-Arab; no white enjoyed any superiority over a black, for superiority is related solely to one's religiosity and God-fearingness.

About two and a half months after delivering this sermon, the Prophet passed away. The problem that arose after his death concerned the choice of his successor. According to the declaration made in the sermon, what should have been done was to decide upon a successor to the caliphate on the basis of piety and God-fearingness, rather than on the basis of family and tribe. But this did not happen.

After his death Muslims gathered at a meeting place in Madinah known as Thaqifa bani Sāida. The majority were of the opinion that Saad ibn Ubada, who belonged to a Madinan tribe, should be selected as the successor to the Prophet. On this occasion Abu Bakr conveyed the Prophet's dictum:

"The leaders will be from the Quraysh."

That is, the Caliph or Imam should be selected from the tribe of the Quraysh. This meant that Saad ibn abi Ubadah, not being a member of that tribe, could not be chosen as caliph. After some deliberation, this issue was finally resolved by deciding that only a member of the Quraysh tribe should be appointed as the Prophet's successor. Accordingly, Abu Bakr, who belonged to the Quraysh tribe, was appointed as first caliph.

There was an apparent contradiction in this. Why should the Prophet ever have made such an observation? There was, however great wisdom behind it. That is, the caliph, or the ruler, having to impose commands on a vast society, required of necessity, that people should be willing to submit to or obey him. Obedience had to be voluntary, for ensuring submission by force would have failed to achieve the aim of the Islamic Caliphate.

In ancient Arabia over the centuries, the Quraysh had come to acquire the position of leadership, so that the public readily accepted the leadership of a person who belonged to this tribe. That was why the Prophet indicated his preference for a Quraysh as his successor. This was not a command of an eternal nature. This meant only that in any community or nation it should be a member of a group which enjoyed a political status such as that of the Quraysh, who should be appointed as its ruler.

This shows that pragmatism was also one of the

sunnah of the Prophet. In individual matters, one should always keep before one what is ideal, but at the same time bear in mind that in social matters sometimes the ideal is not practicable. It is necessary, therefore, that in such matters the ideal be abandoned in favour of practical solutions. If this principle were not observed, the smooth functioning of any given system would not at times be possible.

Future Vision

After the victory of Makkah there followed the year of delegations. The Arabian tribes thronged Madinah to embrace Islam, the tribe of the Thaqif of Taif being one of them. It set a strong precedent for entering the fold of Islam. They said, however, that although they wanted to accept Islam, they would neither pay *zakat* nor perform *jihad.*

It was a serious matter. The Muslims were not willing to accept conditions of this kind. Rising above the present, the Prophet of Islam looked at the future. His deep insight showed that once those people became a part of Muslim society after having embraced Islam, they would surely accept everything on their own, as required by Islam. Therefore, the Prophet accepted their conditions and allowed them to enter his fold. To remove the doubts of his companions, the Prophet said:

"Once they accept Islam, they will pay zakat and perform jihad as well." (Seerat *ibn Kathir*, 4/56)

This example set by the Prophet is illustrative of his great wisdom. This was seeing into the future. Humans are not made of stones. They are open to influence. Man is a creature who keeps changing. His future is different from his present. This reality must always be kept in view while dealing with him. Insisting on instant change produces haughtiness. Whereas, if an attitude of broad-mindedness is adopted, the potential convert will of his own become in future what we wanted to see him turn into in the present.

The Policy of the Prophet

It is generally believed that the way of the Prophet is always to follow the ideal path, rather than make concessions. But this notion is not all-embracing. When in search of practical methods, what is actually worthy of consideration is the situation and circumstances rather than an absolute ideal. The importance of idealism in Islam is no doubt as great as that of making concessions. But neither of these courses is superior to the other in any absolute sense. A study of *seerah* substantiates this point of view.

The word '*Azimat*' does not appear in the Qur'an in the sense of idealism as is generally believed. This word has been used in the Qur'an in the sense of persevering steadfastly, and for refraining from impulsive retaliation. It is never used in the sense of rushing headlong to confront the enemy at every provocation. This is borne out by the following verse:

"Therefore, patiently persevere as did the steadfast apostles before you. And do not seek to hurry on their (i.e. the unbelievers) doom." (46:35)

Here, it is quite clear that the way of patience has been called the way of 'Azimat.' That is to say, despite the provocation, persecution, and other antagonistic activities of opponents, the *dayee* has to exercise patience unconditionally, and to refrain completely from retaliatory activities. This is the way of patience–the way of resolve and courage.

What does making a concession mean? It is not another name for cowardice or escapism. It is in actual fact a strategy, which is resorted to in order to open up better opportunities. In no way does it mean inaction. At the end of the Prophet's stay in Makkah, armed enemies had surrounded the Prophet's house with the avowed intention of killing him. Yet the Prophet did not confront them. Instead, what he did was to leave his home quietly, in the dead of night, and go away to Madinah.

It was not as it might appear, escapism or the taking of an easy course. It was, in actual fact, adherence to a realistic rather than to an emotional plan. Seeking martyrdom on such occasions is not the ideal action, nor is it an act of bravery; it is indeed, an unwise, and futile act. That is why the Prophet scrupulously avoided unnecessary clashes so that he might continue his *dawah* mission all the more effectively. Islam does not call for beheadings; it calls rather for saving the head. Islam does not teach us to annihilate life; it teaches us rather to devote our lives to a good cause.

Islam is a natural religion, with realism as one of its important teachings. The policy of the Prophet of Islam may well be termed a form of pragmatism. In this matter, Islam grants so many concessions that one can even resort to saying something which is not in accordance with the facts in order to save one's life. Saving one's life by some untrue utterance under compulsion is better than showing undue inflexibility and losing one's life futilely as a result of uncalled for fervour for sticking to the "truth."

An incident which took place during the Makkan period is an extreme example. It concerned one Ammar ibn Yasir, who was at that time a slave of an idolatrous Makkan chief. During the Makkan period those believers who were 'freed people' (Makkan society being divided into freed people and slaves) remained largely safe from the oppression of the idolaters, for their tribe protected them. But those who belonged to the slave class, fell victim to severe persecution at the hands of their masters on account of their conversion.

Ammar ibn Yasir was one such convert. His master tortured him and said that unless he expressed his belief in the tribe's idols and denied Muhammad, he would continue to torture him. Under duress, Ammar uttered the words which his idolatrous master wanted to hear. Then Ammar came to the Prophet and said he had uttered those blasphemous words under duress. The Prophet asked him what the true state of his mind was. Ammar replied that his heart was fully convinced of the truth of Islam. Then the Prophet said:

> *"If the idolaters force you to say those words again, you may utter them again."* (Tafsir *ibn Kathir*, 2/587-88)

According to Islam, the Prophet of Islam serves as an example for all humanity. (33:21) In this capacity, it was essential that he lead a life in the world as a human being, undergoing all those states that common people passed through in normal circumstances. If an angel had been placed at his command at all times, so that he could meet the challenges posed to him on a superhuman level, then he could not have served as an example for the common man. In such a situation it would have amounted to asking people to do something which was beyond their capacity. It would have been like asking them to follow a Prophet who was not like them—a Prophet who was possessed of superhuman power. That was why the Prophet, throughout his life, took into account what in normal circumstances was practicable for people and what was not. He conducted his life, according to what was possible and practicable, and refrained from such actions as he thought were impossible for the average person to emulate.

Verbal Dawah

There are always two ways to solve a problem. One way is to plan one's moves by making allowance for practical imperatives. Another way is to rush headlong into things without caring about the result. A study of the 23-year prophetic life of the Prophet shows that the Prophet opted exclusively for the former course.

For instance, 360 idols were ensconced in the Kabah (the house of God). Although the Prophet's mission was to remove them, he never attempted to smash them during his 13-year stay in Makkah after receiving his prophethood. Twenty years thus passed (13 in Makkah, 7 in Madinah), without his having taken any action, for throughout this period the Prophet confined himself only to verbal *dawah*. It was only twenty years later, when Makkah had been conquered, that he took practical steps to purify the Kabah of these idols.

This shows that the Prophet drew a line between what was practicable and what was not. For twenty years verbal *dawah* alone was acceptable as far as idols were concerned. If the Prophet was able to continue his mission, it was because he confined himself to the field of peaceful *dawah*. After the conquest of Makkah, when the purification of the Kabah became feasible, the Prophet took concrete steps towards this end. This shows that differentiating between result-oriented action and non-result-oriented action is also an important *sunnah* of the Prophet.

The Principle of Differentiation

From a study of the Prophet's life, we learn an important principle—that of differentiation. That is to say, understanding significant distinctions in practical matters, and dealing with them accordingly.

This differentiation is a principle of nature and the course followed by the Prophet of Islam bears out the fact that he made full concession to it.

One of the distinctions to be made is between word and deed. For instance, these words of the Prophet have been recorded in a *Hadith:*

> *"The greatest* jihad *was to say a word of truth and justice to a tyrant ruler. (Sunnan abi Dawood, 4/122)*

On the other hand, a number of traditions have been recorded in books of Hadith which show that even if rulers became tyrants, Muslims had to obey them, and never clash with them or adopt a policy of confrontation. (*Mishkat al Masabih,* 3/1484)

For instance, Huzaifa, a companion of the Prophet has been recorded as saying that the Prophet said,

"In later times perversion will set in in the rulers whose bodies will appear to be those of human beings, while their hearts will be those of Satans."

Huzaifa then asked the Prophet what they were supposed to do at such times. The Prophet replied,

"You must pay heed to your ruler and obey him. Even if you are flogged on your back, and your wealth is taken away from you, you must hear and obey him." (Sahih *Muslim, 12/238*)

Let us make a comparative study of these two traditions. In the first Hadith we are encouraged to perform *jihad* against the tyrant ruler, whereas in the second Hadith we are strictly forbidden to do so. The reason for this difference is that the first Hadith relates to verbal advice while the second Hadith relates to practical confrontation. According to the Hadith, verbal advice is a desirable act, while practical confrontation is a totally undesirable act.

Here verbal advice does not mean issuing statements in newspapers, making speeches and staging protests. It only means that when one finds some perversion in a ruler, one should pray for him, and meet him by appointment in private and try to make him understand his shortcomings in total sincerity and with expressions of well-wishing.

When Abdullah ibn Abbas asked the Prophet

will be no more than his personal choice, and his actions will not serve as a model for others.

The way Umar undertook his journey was justified by its being a personal or individual action, but the position of the Prophet of Islam was not merely that of an individual. The Prophet was the leader of the entire Muslim community. His each and every step served as an example for the entire *ummah*. Whatever he did was to be followed by the Muslims for all time, therefore, when it is a question of taking the initiative at the communal level, the same way would be adopted as that of the Prophet at the time of his emigration. That is, before taking any action, all precautions should be taken and full concessions made to the situation and circumstances.

The principle we derive from this incident of the Prophet's emigration is that if someone on his own personal basis, wanted to take a dangerous step, he would be allowed to do so. However, there is no doubt about it that an individual's taking such a step would remain a matter of option or concession and not one of compulsion.

But where a group or community is concerned, taking risky steps with no thought for the result is not allowed by Islam. Moreover, the individual enjoys this right solely in his own personal sphere. He is not allowed to instigate people to engage in emotional and ill-considered actions by means of provocative speeches and writings.

When an individual enjoys the position of a leader, he has to give proper consideration to the interests of the community. Even if he is not a leader, he has no right to incite people by his pen and speeches to adopt a course which might imperil them. He may take such a step in his individual capacity but he is in no circumstances allowed to lead unwary people into danger.

The Example of Husain

We do not find any examples in the life of the Prophet of his taking an emotional step without caring for the consequences. However, there are some people who justify their own stand on the taking of such steps by citing the example of Husain, the grandson of the Prophet. They maintain that the military strength of Imam Husain was far less than that of the Umayyad forces, yet when he saw that truth was not being upheld, the forces of evil being rampant, he battled with the forces of Yazid, without considering the consequences, and sacrificed his life for the cause.

But this image of Husain ibn Ali, being man-made, is totally unrealistic. It is one promoted by poets and orators, for no authentic history presents this picture of Husain ibn Ali. Authentic records—History of Tabari, History of Ibn Kathir, and Al-Bidayah wa-al-Nihayah by ibn Kathir—have all clearly, and in no uncertain terms, stated that when

Husain reached Kufa and was informed of the real situation, he was prepared to go back to Makkah.

The events tell us that when Husain ibn Ali set off from Makkah to Kufa, he had no intention of fighting the forces of Yazid. He was accompanied only by about 150 people, including women, children and even sick people. No one who goes out to do battle would be accompanied by such a group. The only reason for his leaving Makkah for Kufa was that he had received a message from its inhabitants that he should visit their town, as they were all ready to make him their leader. It was on this basis that Husain had gone there.

Albidayah wa al-Nihayah (Part VIII) describes this incident in great detail. From this we learn that when Husain had almost reached Karbala, he received the news that his representative, Muslim ibn Aqil, had been killed by the Umayyad ruler and that, out of fear, the Kufans had withdrawn their allegiance to Husain. At this point Husain decided to go back to Makkah.

According to authentic historical records, the Umayyad army in Kufa did not let him turn back. They wanted to kill him. According to Tabari and other historians, Husain said to the Umayyad governor: "O Umar, accept one of three conditions: Either allow me to go back to where I came from; or if this is not acceptable to you, then take me to Yazid (the caliph) and I will place my hand on his hand and let him decide about me; and if even this is not acceptable, then let me go to the heathen Turks so that I may perform *jihad* against them until I am martyred." The truth is that, justifying what was a self-made political *jihad* in the name of Husain ibn Ali had nothing to do with the actual example set by Husain, and resulted in a distorted version of his true character and actions. Only from authentic historical records may the real picture of Husain be pieced together.

Status Quoism

One very important principle of the Prophet's policy was status quoism, that is, accepting the prevailing situation. However, the status quoism of the Prophet did not simply mean to accept the extant sets of circumstances for all time. It meant rather carving out a path for oneself by adopting a non-confrontational policy within the existing set-up. Far from leading to a state of inertia, this was a planned course of action.

The Prophet of Islam followed this principle in his life at Makkah as well as at Madinah. This is one of the reasons for his achieving such great success— within the short period of 23 years— as had never been achieved by anyone throughout the entire course of human history.

The great benefit of such status quoism is that, by adopting this policy, one is instantly able to avail of opportunities for carrying out one's projects. One is in a position to utilize one's energies fully in one's mission without wasting one iota of effort. By avoiding unnecessary clash and confrontation, one is able to devote oneself to constructive activity to the fullest extent.

The mission of the prophet of Islam was to establish monotheism *(Tawheed)*. When he received his prophethood, the situation in Makkah was that 360 idols were in position inside the Kabah. The presence of these idols in the house of monotheism went totally against his mission. But the Prophet completely refrained from any practical confrontation with the worshippers of these idols, and devoted himself to the propagation of monotheism in theory.

That is, he adopted the principle of status quoism in the matter of the Kabah. The benefit deriving from this policy was the opportunity to communicate the message of monotheism for a period of thirteen years. During these thirteen years he was highly successful in that he managed to bring the 200 most worthy individuals of Makkah within his fold. It was these people, who, by giving their full support to the Prophet, brought the history of Islam into existence.

At the end of the Makkan period the Prophet's uncle Abu Talib died. As he had been the chief of the Banu Hashim, his death left the Prophet without the kind of support, he needed to lead his life under that tribal system. Here too the Prophet, taking advantage of the situation in Makkah, managed to find a supporter in Mutim ibn Adi. As we know, Mutim ibn Adi was an idolater. But the Prophet, welcomed his support, for there was scope for this in terms of status quo in Arabia.

After the emigration when he reached Madinah, he found idolaters and Jews living alongside Muslims. But in order to establish a system based on Islamic teachings, the Prophet did not immediately attempt to launch a movement to expel Jews and idolaters from Madinah. Instead, he announced the establishment of a system based on the existing society. This declaration is called the charter of Madinah. It was mentioned in this Charter that the affairs of their tribes would be settled according to whichever of their own traditions were prevalent at the time.

The Prophet Ibrahim (and later Ismail) had established the Hajj system on the basis of the lunar calendar, which is of a shorter duration than the solar calendar. The idolaters subsequently adjusted the calendar to the solar system. The Prophet of Islam was then entrusted by God with changing back to the lunar calendar. But the Prophet neither attempted to bring about this change during his stay in Makkah, nor did he even broach the subject immediately after the conquest of Makkah. He waited for almost the whole of his life before he took this step. He did so only in the 23rd year of his prophethood, when in accordance with astronomical principles, the Hajj fell on the correct date of *Dhul Hijjah,* as in the system established by Ibrahim. This was when the Prophet performed his last 'farewell' pilgrimage, and on this occasion the Prophet announced that, in future, Hajj would always be performed in the month of Dhul Hijjah. (For further details, see the book, *Muhammad, A Prophet for All Humanity,* by the author, p.95 in the chapter entitled, "The Revolution of the Prophet.")

This status quoism abounds in the life of the Prophet of Islam, to the extent that some matters were left in their existing state, although the Prophet knew fully, well that after him no one would be able to change them.

One clear example of this is provided by the issue of *Hateem* (an unbuilt area) in the Kabah. When the Prophet Ibrahim and Ismail built their mosque in the form of the Kabah, it included the part known as Hateem. Originally, the Kabah built by Ibrahim was rectangular while the present Kabah is a square. This square Kabah was built by the idolators. Once the ancient walls of the Kabah collapsed in the wake of a flood, and then were rebuilt. But, due to the shortage of building material, the Quraysh could cover only half of the area, the other half being left unbuilt. Aisha, the wife of the Prophet, said that the Prophet had told her that he wanted to bring down the present walls of the Kabah and re-build them on the foundation laid by Ibrahim. But since the people had recently converted, he feared that they would be provoked at such a step. Therefore, the Prophet left the Kabah on the existing foundations. That meant that the Kabah would remain forever on the foundations laid by the idolaters. (*Fathul Bari,* 3/513)

There are many such instances which go to show that the method of the Prophet of Islam was to proceed carefully without upsetting the status quo, rather than go on a collision course with a long-established convention.

The Prophet of Islam and other Prophets

We find from the Qur'an and *Hadith* that a large number of God's messengers were sent to different nations and regions. The majority of these Prophets are unknown from the historical point of view. It is because the books written by these messengers' contemporaries make no mention of them or their work. It is as if to these chroniclers the prophets and the incidents connected with them were not worthy of being mentioned.

For instance the Prophet Ibrahim was born in Iraq, the Prophet Moses was born in Egypt, and the Prophet Christ was born in Palestine, yet the ancient histories of the respective countries make no reference to them. This was the case with all the past prophets. These messengers were believed in as a matter of creed, without their ever having been established as personalities from the historical standpoint.

Some of these prophets find mention in the Bible. But in a sacred book this goes by belief and not according to historical records.

The characters of Muhammad's predecessors have been presented in such a distorted way that, if biblical statements were taken to be correct, it would be hard to believe that they were indeed God's apostles. According to the picture painted in the Bible, they were not superior models, especially from the ethical point of view. One very important feature of the Qur'an is that it has restored those chapters in the lives of the past prophets which had been lost to the people, because they had gone unrecorded.

Without doubt the prophets are examples of the loftiest human character. But because of the unscientific methods of history-writing which prevailed in their times only events connected with kings, royalty and generals were considered worthy of being recorded, thus depriving posterity of precious details of the lives of the prophets. The Qur'an opened this closed chapter for the first time in history.

But to what end? It might seem that a recital of the facts relating to the life and mission of the Prophet of Islam would have sufficed. But there was a very good reason for making frequent mention of these prophets individually, and also testifying to their having received God's guidance, a blessing which exalted them above all other creatures. It was so that the Prophet of Islam and his *Ummah* might learn valuable lessons from the ways in which these prophets dealt with their circumstances and the situations in which they found themselves.

In the Qur'an, the Prophet of Islam is thus addressed:

> *"These are whom Allah guided aright, so follow their guidance." (6:91)*

Every one of them was an upright man guided by God along a straight path and as such was superior to all others. Chapter 6 mentions a number of these prophets by name. They are: Ibrahim, Ishaaq, Yaqub, Noah, Dawood, Sulaiman, Ayyub, Yousuf, Musa, Haroon, Zakariya, Isa, Ismail, Al-Yasa, Younus, and Lot, (Peace be upon them).

In the fifth chapter, mentioning the earlier prophets and their communities, the Qur'an further clarifies this point:

> *We have ordained a law and a path for each of you (5:48).*

The crux of this matter is that although God's religion is one—monotheism—the human condition keeps changing, individually as well as socially.

That is why, despite there being one single religion, its practical application varies with circumstances. This is what accounts for the dissimilarity of approach on the part of different prophets. Then the human race is spread all over the world, while each respective prophet, including the Prophet of Islam, came from one particular region. That is why it was impossible for one prophet to experience all the possible contingencies which, on a vaster level, would subsequently affect the human race at different times and places. These are the special considerations, which account for the mention of the past prophets in the Qur'an at length.

When we have before us all the prophets, it becomes possible to draw on examples pertinent to all sets of circumstances faced by each generation in turn. This is the main purpose of the Qur'an in bringing these lost links of the history of the prophets to the knowledge of succeeding generations. In this respect the analysis of the incidents arising from the circumstances in which these Prophets lived is an integral part of what is called in the Qur'an (completion of religion) *takmeel-e-din.*(5:3)

The difference of *Minhaj* or *shariah*–each Prophet was given a different Shariah (detailed code of conduct/laws)–with each succeeding prophet is not on account of evolution. That is, it is not true to say that the earlier prophets were given an incomplete *shariah,* while the final Prophet was given the complete *shariah.* This difference is due to a variety of factors in the application of Islam and not to the evolution of the religion itself. Since social environments in the times of successive prophets were different, the *shariah* given to them had to relate to their circumstances. Were those past situations to prevail once again, the *shariah* of the previous prophets would be followed as was done is their times.

On the one hand, the Qur'an gives us an account of the 23 year prophetic life of the Prophet of Islam, while on the other, it also recounts in detail the lives and circumstances of other prophets who came over the last tens of thousands of years. Both these accounts (the Prophet of Islam's life and circumstances and those of other prophets) equally form part of the Qur'an and their combination constitutes the complete religion. Thus a complete *din* includes the teachings of other prophets along with the teachings of the Prophet of Islam as mentioned in the Qur'an. After this introduction let us see in the light of certain examples how references to other prophets form part of the totality of religion and how they provide guidance to believers in different sets of circumstances.

Such examples are to be found in the times of the Prophet Adam, who was the first man as well as the first prophet. We find from the Qur'an that Adam had two sons, Cain and Abel. Cain quarreled violently with Abel and matters escalated to the point where he became intent on killing his own brother. On this occasion, Abel, the virtuous brother, has been recorded in the Qur'an as having said:

*"If you stretch out your hand to kill me, I shall
not lift mine to slay you." (5:28)*

From this we learn the *shariah* based on the
example (*uswah*) set by a virtuous person who had
received guidance from the first prophet. This shows
that among the believers, mutual strife is totally
forbidden. If at times the believers reach a point of
head-on clash and confrontation, it is the virtuous
one who refrains from killing his brother and who
risks being killed.

This example is borne out by the teachings of the
Prophet of Islam himself. According to a tradition the
Prophet totally forbade fighting or even confrontation
amongst Muslims. Once a certain person asked the
Prophet how, if a Muslim were intent on killing him,
he should react to this. The Prophet replied:

*"You should be the better of the two sons of
Adam." (*Mishkat Al-Masabih, *3/1486*)

A practical example of this *shariah* of the first
Prophet, endorsed by the Prophet of Islam, can be
seen in the life of Usman, the third Caliph. When a
group of Muslims came to kill him, despite all the
power he had at his disposal, he did not give
permission for arms to be taken up against the
insurgents.

As regards the Prophet Abraham in the Qur'an,
the believers are told that "you have a 'good example'

in Ibrahim and those who followed him." (60:4). There are many aspects to this good example. Here we shall mention only one.

We find from a prayer offered by Abraham that the culture prevalent in his times had totally corrupted people's minds. As a result of worshipping false gods for several centuries, they had allowed these deities to become a part of their unconscious minds. It had become almost impossible for a person born in these urban centres of idol worship to keep himself untainted by this corrupting influence (14:36).

At this juncture, the Prophet Abraham devised a historic plan of founding a new generation, a step which has no precedent in ancient history. According to this plan, the Prophet Abraham settled Ismail and his mother Hajira in a desert in Arabia. It was at that time an uninhabited valley far away from the centres of civilization. Here the environment was totally natural. Thus it was possible to raise a generation, cut off from the atmosphere of idolatrous civilization, which would retain its God-given nature intact.

Abraham's plan fructified and when Ismael grew up, he married a virtuous lady of a Bedouin tribe. With this union, the generation desired by God began to take shape in this desert world. In this atmosphere there were only two things required for intellectual training–internal human nature and the outer universe created by God "with Truth." (14:19)

In this healthy and favourable atmosphere

generation succeeded generation over a long period of two thousand five hundred years. This culminated in the final Prophet being raised among these people. His was a historic generation which produced those high-calibre individuals, noble souls known as the *sahaba*, the Prophet's companions, numbering about one lakh. The Qur'an calls them 'the best people,' while certain orientalists have called them a "community of heroes" in view of the extraordinary feats performed by them.

This example of the Prophet Abraham shows that in any age where the corruption of an evil civilization predominates, and it appears that the people living in that atmosphere will not be able to remain aloof from the general perversion of values, the only course is to find a safe haven far away from bad influences. These special arrangements may be made for the training and education of children and young people.

If this plan is properly carried out, as the history of the Prophets Ibrahim and Ismail tells us, this training centre of nature may once again produce such noble souls as are well-equipped to change the course of history, so that it may be re-directed along healthier lines.

Another incident which pertains to a prophet is recounted in the Qur'an. It concerned the Prophet Yunus, who was sent to communicate the message of monotheism to the idolaters of Nineveh, an ancient city of Iraq. After doing *Dawah* work there for a period of time, he felt that his hearers were not going to believe in God's message, and so deserved divine punishment for their denial of monotheism. Arriving at this conclusion on his own, he left Nineveh.

The people of Ninevah remained unaffected, while the Prophet Yunus was swallowed up by a whale. He suddenly found himself in the whale's belly, and there was no way out of this plight.

What was the reason behind this? The reason was that a community may be adjudged deniers of monotheism only when they have had the message of *dawah* conveyed to them in full. A lack of success after performing *dawah* work for only a limited period of time does not warrant the stigmatizing of a people as deniers of God's message.

Therefore, when the Prophet Yunus found himself in the whale's belly, he gave himself up to introspection. Then it was revealed to him that he had abandoned his people before the completion of his task. The *sunnah* (way) of the prophets is that they leave their people only after the *dawah* work has reached its completion. When he realized his mistake, he sought forgiveness from God and prayed. God granted his prayer. The whale then brought him to a dry land and regurgitated him. After this, Prophet Yunus came back to his people and began calling them again to the path of monotheism. This time, almost all of his people entered the fold of the religion of monotheism.

Such an event as relating to a prophet has an extremely important lesson for believers. This incident has been thus described in the Qur'an:

> *A whale swallowed him, for he had erred; and had he not devoutly praised Allah, he would have stayed in its belly till the Day of Resurrection. (37:142-144)*

This goes to show how great is the responsibility of *dawah*. Those who fail to discharge this duty properly, are destined according to the law of God, to find themselves "in the whale's belly." And they will never be saved from this great ordeal until they repent and return to perform *dawah* work. Otherwise they will remain in that plight until Doomsday. If we ponder on this, we find that this example applies in all respects to the Muslim *Ummah*. Such are their problems that the Muslim *Ummah* has been engulfed in the belly of the whale for more than a hundred years. Countless attempts and innumerable sacrifices in terms of wealth and precious lives have not succeeded in leading them out of this quandary. When looked at in the light of this *sunnah* of the Prophet, the only reason we can find for their being in this plight is that the *Ummah* has abandoned *dawah* work for a very long period of time. The Muslims have reached a stage where they have no idea of how *dawah* is to be performed. They engage themselves in community work while calling it *dawah*. There is only one way for them to come out of the "belly of the whale" and that is to sincerely admit how mistaken has been their total negligence of the duty of *dawah*. This would be an act of repentance on their part. The whole *ummah* must engage themselves in performing *dawah* work anew throughout the nations of the world and, if they are to fulfill all its conditions, they shall have to bring their task to completion.

The Qur'an repeatedly mentions events concerning the Prophet Moses. Without doubt there are many lessons in his life for the believers. Here I would like to mention one lesson which I have personally experienced.

I have been working for Islamic *dawah* since 1948. But in the early days I was not able to speak out (or make an extempore speech) to an audience. Therefore, I used to write my speeches and then read them out. If I had no written speech in front of me, my heart trembled and I began to shake, unable to express myself.

This was the situation for about fifteen years. It had become an accepted fact that I did not speak impromptu at gatherings, but only read out papers. It was only in 1962 that I reached the stage of being able to speak extempore in public.

In 1962 the Jama'at-i-Islami had organized a monthly public meeting at Anjan Shaheed, a town in Azamgarh, U.P. I too was to address this gathering. However, contrary to my habit, I did not put my speech down in writing. When my turn came to deliver a speech, I stood up and recalled the prayer made by Moses and its answer from God. I uttered these words in a frenzied, emotional state. "The Qur'an is not a book of history. It is a living guidance. The incidents and events mentioned in it are as relevant for us as they were for the personalities of the past referred to, in the Qur'an." Then after recounting the story of Moses, I said: "If a servant of God finds himself helpless in making a speech and he calls to God for help in the words of Moses:

> 'Lord, I fear they will reject me. I may become impatient and stammer in my speech.' (26:13), I am certain that he will receive the same answer as was received by Moses: "Granted is your prayer, O Moses."

This incident marked a turning point in my life. From that time onwards, all my hesitancy in speech was gone and I began to address large gatherings without any diffidence. This is a personal example of the great lesson we have in the life of the Prophet Moses. And there are many other lessons in his life which will serve as a guide to believers right till Doomsday.

Similarly, the Qur'an repeatedly mentions Christ. There are many examples in his life and teachings for the believers, one such example being an observation made by him to his disciples:

"But I say to you who hear: Love your enemies, do good to those who hate you. Bless those who curse you, and pray for those who spitefully use you. To him who strikes you on the one cheek, offer the other also. And from him who takes away your cloak, do not withhold your tunic either. Give to everyone who asks of you. And from him who takes away your goods, do not ask them back." (Luke 6:27:30).

Christ has not taught us passivity in these words. This is in actual fact a part of *dawah* etiquette. A *dayee* must always possess good behaviour unconditionally. If he were to indulge in retaliation, the normal, favourable atmosphere essential for the performance of *dawah* would vanish altogether.

The *sunnah* of the Prophet of Islam testifies to this. Let us take an incident relating to Suhaib Rumi, who migrated from Makkah to Madinah after most of the Muslims had left Makkah. Some way out of the city, a group of Quraysh youths blocked his path. They told him that they would not let him go with all the earnings he had made in Makkah. Suhaib had a few *dinars* (gold coins) with him at that time. He asked them:

"If I let you have these dinars, will you let me go?"

They said that they would. Suhayb then gave all his money to them and carried on to Madinah. When Suhaib reached Madinah and the Prophet heard about this incident, he said:

"Suhayb has profited! Suhayb has profited."
(Seerah ibn Hisham, *2/89*).

The truth is that the ethics preached by Christ to his disciples apply equally to the believers. These are the salient prerequisites of *dawah* which the *dayee* has to adopt in the case of the *madu.* If a moral code of this nature is not adhered to unilaterally, the *dawah* process can never even be initiated.

The Prophet Yusuf is the only one of the prophets whose story takes up a whole chapter (entitled Yusuf). His story concludes with these words: "That which we now reveal to you is a tale of the unknown... Assuredly, in its narrative is a lesson for men of understanding." (12:103, 112). That is to say that it was a lost chapter of history which had been opened by God, so that the believers might learn from it.

Moreover, near the end of the story, we are told in the words of Prophet Yusuf that "Those who keep from evil and endure with fortitude, will never be denied their reward by Allah" (12:90). This shows that the character of Prophet Yusuf exemplifies the principle of *taqwa* (piety) and *sabr* (patience). By that token wherever the principles of *taqwa* and *sabr* are implemented, they will certainly yield the desired result.

In this narration of the Prophet Yusuf there are many lessons to be learnt. Here I would like to mention one in particular. The story unfolds in Egypt which was ruled at that time by an idolatrous king. Yusuf entered this kingdom as a slave and was later imprisoned for purely non-political reasons. Subsequently a dream which the Pharaoh had, brought about a revolutionary change in the state of affairs. Impressed by Yusuf's interpretation of his dream, he offered him a post in his government which, in today's jargon, might be termed the Food and Agriculture Minister. Since this was an agricultural age, when the national economy was based on agriculture, this post had become the most important of all the departments of the kingdom. Therefore, in actuality, Yusuf came to assume the position of prime minister in the state.

This aspect of the matter is extremely important, for the Prophet Yusuf was certainly a *dayee* of *tauhid* (monotheism) (12:39). Despite this he accepted a subsidiary post under the patronship of an idolatrous King of Egypt. His doing so may have appeared inappropriate. But according to the Qur'an itself, it was a matter of *taqwa* and *sabr* in the full sense of these words.

In this we find an important principle of the religion of monotheism. That is to say that being a monotheist does not mean that in practical matters, no partnership can be formed with those who are not monotheists. *Tauhid* does not demand that the confrontation must continue between monotheists and non-monotheists until the non-monotheists are given a death blow, surrendering complete power into the hands of monotheists. The example of the Prophet Yusuf clearly refutes the validity of such a concept. On the contrary, the truth is that while adhering steadfastly to belief in monotheism, in one's personal life we must adopt the policy of adjustment and partnership with others in practical and social affairs.

If we look deeper, we will find that in present times, the sufferings Muslims are facing in every country are mostly due to their ignorance of this *sunnah* of the Prophet Yusuf. In present times, there is every possibility for Muslim religious leaders, by accepting the sovereignty of the Muslim rulers in their own countries, to deal with them on the basis of partnership.

Similarly, in countries with non-Muslim majorities, Muslims may benefit from any democratic set-up which is based on a system of power-sharing. If the Muslim leaders of modern times had accepted this fact, extraordinary opportunities for progress would have opened up for Muslims in every country. But our Muslim leaders have adopted the politics of confrontation all over the world. This is a clear deviation from the *sunnah* of the Prophet, which will result in nothing in this life and in the Hereafter. These few illustrations go to show that there are very precious examples for believers in the lives and teachings of the other prophets mentioned in the Qur'an. We must therefore adopt these *sunnahs* as being as reliable as the examples set by the Prophet of Islam.

Sunnah Hudaybiya

After the Prophet of Islam received prophethood he worked to propagate the message of monotheism for the initial period of thirteen years in Makkah. Makkah was his hometown, but the Makkans turned his direst enemies. They inflicted all sorts of persecution upon him and ultimately they decided to kill him in order to remove him from their path. At this juncture the Prophet and his companions left Makkah for Madinahat the command of God. This amounted to being exiled, for, apparently, there was no hope of the Makkan people ever letting him enter Makkah again. It was under such difficult circumstances that the Prophet had a dream in Madinahthat he, along with his companions, was entering Makkah peacefully and was freely performing *umrah* (minor pilgrimage) sacrifices.

In accordance with this dream the Prophet and his 1500 companions set off for Makkah from Madinah on the first of *Dhu Al-Qada in* 6 A.H. As this caravan headed towards Makkah everyone felt great excitement. But when it reached a place known as Hudaybiya near Makkah, the Makkans stopped them from going forward. They said that at all costs they would prevent the Muslims from entering Makkah.

The Prophet and his companions stayed at Hudaybiya for two weeks. During this period negotiations went on and, finally it was settled that the Prophet and his companions would not enter Makkah that year. Instead they were to return from Hudaybiya to Madinah, and come the following year for a stay of only three days, during which they were to quietly perform *umra* and then go back without delay. According to this treaty the Prophet and his companions, in spite of the Prophet's dream, left Hudaybiya for Madinah. The following year they came again and performed *umra* as stipulated by the treaty of Hudaybiya.

This incident of Hudaybiya tells us a special *sunnah* of the Prophet, that is, not clashing with others unnecessarily; refraining scrupulously from turning any difficult situation into a prestige issue; rather taking the problem as it is and keeping oneself free from any complexes; attempting to understand matters by rising above sentiments and emotions, and solving problems wisely by giving concessions to the other party.

This policy can also be termed status quoism. This does not simply mean accepting the status quo without attempting to change it. Status quoism is not passivity or inaction, but rather the highest form of action. Whenever a confrontational situation builds up between two parties, the controversy comes to a standstill at a certain point. Now apparently there is only one way to proceed for both the parties, and that is, to break the status quo and find a way to go ahead.

On such occasions, the foolish turn such matters into a prestige issue. They believe that accepting the status quo would amount to losing face. To protect their egos they take to the path of confrontation. But one who is God-fearing never turns anything into a prestige issue. *Taqwa* for him becomes a guarantee of keeping himself away from any such confrontation as will result in nothing but destruction.

When the individual refrains from making a controversial matter into one of prestige, this gives rise to serious thinking. This non-emotional thinking helps him to understand that if he were to walk out of the point of controversy he would find all other paths open to him. The same was the case in Hudaybiya. The Prophet of Islam wanted to enter Makkah but the Quraysh did not allow him to do so. Yet the Prophet did not let the obstructiveness of the *Quraysh* become a matter of prestige. His own positive approach enabled him to lead Muslims away from the field of war to the field of *dawah*, a far vaster arena for their struggle in the cause of Islam.

By unilaterally accepting all the conditions of the opponents of Islam, the Prophet of Islam made a no-war pact called the Hudaybiya Peace Treaty in 6 A.H. On account of his unconditional acceptance of the enemy's terms, some Muslims held it to be a humiliating pact (*Seerah ibn Hisham*, 3/365). But after this treaty was finalized, the chapter in the Qur'an, called 'Victory' (Al-Fath) was revealed, in which this peace treaty was called 'a clear victory.' (48:1)

The reason for this difference in assessment was that human beings looked at it from the angle of the present, while God looked at it from the angle of future. It is this reality which has been pointed out in the Qur'an in these words:

Allah knew what you did not know (48:27)

At its beginning, the Hudaybiya peace treaty appeared to mean nothing but surrender and humiliation. But God saw it from the point of view of its practical result in the future. That is why the Qur'an called it a clear victory. "The well known *taabii,* a disciple of the companions, Ibn Shihab Az Zuhri says:

> *"Never before in Islam had there been such a great victory before Hudaybiya. Whenever Muslims and non-Muslims met one another, before Hudaybiya they came to the point of*

confrontation. But when peace prevailed and war was stopped under the treaty, people became safe from one another. In this peaceful atmosphere, they interacted with one another and began exchanging their thoughts. Then whoever had an occasion to hear about Islam, and had sound judgement, entered its fold. After the peace treaty, within a period of two years, as many people or even more accepted Islam as had done so before, only over a much longer period of time."

Ibn Hisham, the Prophet's biographer, says that *Zuhri's* observation is proved true by the fact that, according to the tradition narrated by *Jabir ibn Abdullah,* there were only 1400 men with the Prophet on his journey to Hudaybiya. But two years after that, when the Prophet set out for the conquest of Makkah, he was accompanied by ten thousand companions.

The Hudaybiya *sunnah* is the sum total of the actions of the Prophet of Islam which resulted in the 'clear victory' as recorded in the Qur'an, which led the Islamic movement to the age of revolution and ultimate ascendancy. Consequently, such opportunities were opened up for Islam as had never hitherto presented themselves. What is Sunnah Hudaybiya? It is, to put it briefly, to ignore the problems in order to buy time in which to avail of the opportunities.

God has made this world in such a way that, here, according to the Qur'an, difficulty is always accompanied by ease (Chapter 103). By the very system or law of nature itself, it happens that in this world there are always favourable opportunities alongside problems. By availing of these opportunities, great progress can be made. The reason for failure in life is often traceable to the fact that people become embroiled in controversy. They think that unless all obstacles and hurdles are removed, the onward journey can never be made.

But the Sunnah of the Prophet of Islam is totally different. That is, one should refrain from tackling difficulties by confrontational methods. Instead we must find ways and means of availing of the existing opportunities by avoiding the problems. If necessary this principle should be observed to the extent of our being willing to accept the unilateral conditions of the opponents, treating them as representing a temporary phase.

The incident that took place in Hudaybiya is a specific instance. Apparently it is regarded as only one of the many such incidents recorded in *seerah*. But, in reality, it is not just one happening like many others. In actual fact, the spirit of Hudaybiya pervades the entire life of the Prophet. It would not be wrong to say that this was a very well-considered policy of the Prophet which he adopted throughout his life.

The Hudaybiya policy, in fact, is that in any set of

circumstances, problems have to be ignored and opportunities, despite all difficulties, have to be availed of. We find a number of examples of this policy in the life of the Prophet. The Prophet followed this same principle in his Makkan as well as Madinan period. The only difference between Hudaybiya and other similar incidents is that on the occasion of Hudaybiya this policy was adopted following a bilateral declaration, while at other times it was followed by a unilateral decision.

The method of the Prophet was to study the prevailing sets of circumstances dispassionately and objectively and then follow that course on his own, without any external pressure. This is what we have called the Hudaybiya policy. For instance, in the early phase in Makkah, the Prophet communicated his *dawah* message secretly. This did not mean that the Prophet had a meeting with the idolaters of Makkah, and then as a matter of bilateral decision-making engaged not to propagate his message publicly but in secret. It was rather that by making concessions to circumstances, he on his own adopted the method of secret propagation, without waiting for any social compulsion.

Similarly, when he gave the call of monotheism publicly, it did not happen that the Prophet and the idolaters of Makkah met and talked about it and then arrived at the decision that the idols placed in Kabah would not be harmed and that the Prophet would disseminate his message by following the peaceful *dawah* method. Rather what happened was that the Prophet himself set this limit for his *dawah* activity. That is he gave the verbal call to abandon the worship of anything other than God, but refrained completely from any practical confrontation with the worshippers of idols placed in the House of God.

Similarly, when the Prophet of Islam reached Madinah, he found Jews also settled there. But he did not first have bilateral exchanges with the Jews and then reach an agreement that the Muslims (living in Madinah) would not force the Jews to adopt their ideology but would permit them to enjoy freedom of religion. Instead, after assessing the situation prevailing in Madinah, the Prophet himself set an acceptable limit for his own missionary work in order not to come into unnecessary clash and confrontation with the Jews. Therefore these words were enshrined in the well-known charter of Madinah. For the Jews, the religion of the Jews, for the Muslims, the religion of the Muslims. (*Seerah ibn Kathir*, 2/322)

The essence of the Hudaybiya spirit is to completely refrain from entering into any controversy with the other party and to concentrate all one's efforts on achieving one's goal in non-controversial fields. This policy can be followed only when the *dayee* is willing to give concessions to the other party unilaterally–the concession which the other party at that point in time considers its right. The Hudaybiya policy cannot be followed without such unilateral concession-making. A study of the *seerah* shows that the Prophet always followed the same policy. That is the reason why it became possible for him to minimize his losses and maximize his benefits.

Al-Furqan is a chapter of the Qur'an which was revealed in Makkah at a time when the Prophet was commanded to perform *dawah* alone, and he used to engage himself day and night in discharging the duty assigned to him. At this stage the Prophet was enjoined in the Qur'an not to "yield to unbelievers, but strive against them with it (the Qur'an) with the utmost strenuousness. (25:52).

The Qur'an does not consist of bombs and bullets. Therefore it is clear that these verses do not speak of armed struggle but of peaceful ideological struggle. This means that *dawah* work is to be performed with the help of the teachings of Islam. We must make the Qur'an understandable to people by exploiting all kinds of peaceful means. People's hearts and minds have to be conquered by the veracity of the Qur'an.

This verse evidently indicates the superiority of *dawah* as compared to armed *jihad*. According to it there are two kinds of *jihad*–minor *jihad* and major *jihad*, armed struggle being the minor *jihad* and peaceful struggle being the major *jihad*.

Hudaybiyah provides a great example of this great *jihad* in the history of Islam. After migration the

Muslims faced an armed onslaught from their opponents. Several armed clashes between the believers and non-believers took place. But these produced no decisive results, for, at that time, the real target was for Makkah to be brought once again into the fold of monotheism: this target could not be realized by all these wars. Ultimately, in the 6th year of *hijrah,* the Prophet of Islam finalized the Hudaybiya peace treaty between the believers and unbelievers. This treaty sought to change the arena of struggle from one of violence to one of peace. Here the Hudaybiya method proved very effective. Within two years of this treaty, Makkah was conquered and the believers found the opportunity to convert the city of Makkah, a city which had become a centre of idolatry for centuries—into a centre of monotheism.

There is great guidance for us in this *sunnah* of the Prophet. Careful study shows that in present times we are faced with the same state of affairs as prevailed at the time of Hudaybiya in the first phase of the Islamic revolution. Here the Prophet's sunnah shows us the way to follow this prophetic policy in today's circumstances and be held deserving by God of a 'clear victory' once again.

The Muslims of present times have waged *jihad* with other nations for more than a hundred years. They have received nothing in return save death and destruction. Now the demand of *sunnah* of the Prophet is to put all such confrontations to an end unilaterally, and engage all our efforts in the positive construction of Islam and Muslims. There is simply no other path to success for present-day Muslims.

The Hudaybiya principle is not jut a *sunnah* in the simple sense of the word. Rather it is an eternal law of nature. If this law were to be put into practice not only by Muslims but also by non-Muslim nations, they would reap the same benefits in their respective fields.

One example of this is provided by modern Japan. By the time of the second world war, Japan was of the view that it could fulfill its national goals by means of military action. But it suffered a severe defeat in this war. Its economy was destroyed. After the war, a new thinking surfaced amongst the Japanese. Removing themselves from the field of war and confrontation they centered all their efforts on the fields of education, commerce and industry. The result of this change was that an annihilated Japan could stand up once again and become an international economic power.

The event of Hudaybiya is explained in the Qur'an in chapter 48 which is called *'al-Fath.* We can understand the Hudaybiya spirit by studying this verse:

When those who disbelieved harboured in their hearts bigotry—the bigotry of Jahiliyya (of the Days of Ignorance), Allah sent down His

tranquillity on His Messenger and on the
believers and made the word of piety binding
on them, for they were most worthy and
deserving of it. Allah has knowledge of all
things. (48:27)

This verse revealed on the occasion of the peace treaty of Hudaybiya, (like other verses of the Qur'an) also has a general and extended application. In this respect we find in it an eternal teaching of Islam, relevant, like other teachings of Islam to all later times.

Looked at from this angle, we find that the point made in this verse is that in the present world, for various reasons, individuals and communities often clash and come into confrontation with one another. This verse of the Qur'an guides us as to what course we must adopt in such situations.

In accordance with this verse, there are only two possible modes of behaviour in such controversial situations, for individuals as well as for nations—one being based on godliness and the other on ungodliness (an insolent attitude). Success is reserved only for those who adopt a god-fearing attitude on such occasions. For those who are fearless of God, nothing but failure awaits them in this world.

What would an ungodly attitude be on such occasions? It is called *hamiyat-e-jahiliyya* in the Qur'an. The truth is that people generally become provoked in a controversial situation. Negative feelings within them are activated. They are not in a position to look at the matter with a cool mind and arrive at a settlement solely on the basis of principle. Those who give in to such a negative attitude fall prey to *hamiyat jahiliya,* as the Qur'an calls it.

The opposite attitude is that which is called god-fearing in the Qur'an. The god-fearing are those who adhere strictly to the path of principled approach for they fear the retribution of Allah. They hold fast to the path of truth and justice, even in the face of extreme provocation. Their judgements and decisions are not the result of reaction, but rather of careful deliberation.

According to the Qur'an, the ungodly attitude as mentioned above is wholly against the spirit of Islam. Those who opt for ungodly ways can never succeed in this world of God. On the contrary those who opt for godly ways will certainly be successful. It is the decree of the Creator of the universe that they will succeed. The incident of Hudaybiya in the first phase of Islam provides a practical example. In this matter one course was that opted for by the non-Muslims of Makkah. The other was that which the believers opted for, in following the leadership of the Prophet. Now in the light of this incident everyone can judge his actions for himself. Those who opt for the ungodly path in the thick of controversy are practically joining the group of non-Muslims, while opting for the godly course in such a situation amounts to joining the body of believers.

Chapter 48 of the Qur'an begins with these words: We have granted you a clear victory. In this context it means that God has decreed victory in this world only for those who adopt a godly attitude, while those who adopt an ungodly course of action are destined to remain in a state of subjugation.

The incident of Hudaybiya provides a historic example of conduct appropriate to the situation. The believers on that occasion, in taking up a godly attitude, entitled themselves to victory, while the Quraysh who took up an ungodly attitude had consequently to suffer defeat and failure.

The incident of Hudaybiya is not simply a chapter of past history. It is a living historical example. It tells believers in every age as to which course in controversial situations is a sure guarantee of success. This involves refraining from making a controversial matter into one of prestige, rather trying to seek a solution in the spirit of *taqwa* (God-fearing spirit).

The Prophetic Mission

What was the goal or mission of the Prophet of Islam? This is indeed a very important question. To determine it academically requires a thorough study of the Qur'an and Sunnah, the sources of Islam. First of all the basic guiding principles must be laid down for such a study.

The first principle is that the correct answer to this question could only be one which is derived directly from the holy scriptures, that is, the Qur'an. No argument of an inferential nature would be at all useful. An inferential, or indirect argument is useful only in matters of a partial or relative nature. But so far as the determining of the mission or goal is concerned (relating to basic issues), inferential argument cannot be employed. For instance, if one argued that the mission of the Prophet of Islam was to establish an Islamic state and in support of this he quoted the following verse of the Qur'an, he would be making a serious error:

"We have sent our Messengers with clear signs and sent down with them the Book and the scales of justice, so that people may act with justice. We have sent down iron, with its mighty strength and diverse uses for mankind, so that Allah may know those who help Him and His messengers without having seen Him. Allah is powerful and Mighty" (57:25)

Suppose someone were to pick out the words 'scales of justice' (or 'balance' as it would be expressed in Arabic) and link it with 'iron' to support his argument that the Islamic mission was to establish justice by using the power of iron (i.e. weaponry), he would not be right in his contention.

This argument is not valid from the academic point of view, for the word 'balance' in the first part of the verse is used to enjoin people to mould their lives to the standard of justice, to be just in their dealings, and to adopt the ways of justice in their own lives; it is not asking them to impose their concept of justice on others.

Thus if someone, by citing this verse, put forward an argument for coercing others, his argument would be academically untenable, because it would be totally illogical.

The second principle is that any concept of the Prophet's mission should be determined on the basis of the fundamental teachings of the Prophet, rather than of later Islamic history. For basic teachings are eternal in their nature, whereas history shapes itself around social or human circumstances.

For instance, there are certain people who hold that the order of the prophetic action is—*dawah, hijrat, jihad,* then the establishment of the state. This amounts to deriving the mission from history. For, at no point do the Qur'an and *Hadith* mention that the eternal order of the Prophetic mission would be to first perform *dawah,* then undertake migration, then perform *jihad* in the sense of doing battle, and then in the fourth stage establish the Islamic state. This order has been derived from a historical sequence of events as they unfolded, rather than from the fundamental teachings of the Qur'an and *Hadith.*

Contrary to this, the Qur'an tells us that the Prophet's mission could have been brought to its completion even if he had passed away or had been killed before the establishment of the state (3:144). It would not be wrong to say in the light of this verse that, even if the Prophet had left the world before the establishment of the State, his prophetic mission would be treated as accomplished. For no prophet is taken away from the world before the completion of his mission.

Another important point is that such series of events are never repeated in history. That is why the above-mentioned four fold order has neither occurred in the case of any of the Prophet's precedessors nor has it been repeated by any subsequent reformer or revivalist.

If this order were to enjoy the position of being inherent in and inseparable from the prophetic mission, Islam would become a temporary religion, relevant only to a particular period of time. For instance, under present-day national governments, mass exodus is not at all possible. In that case how could the act of migration be carried out? Similarly today *jihad*, in the sense of offensive war, is not in practice possible, for now, the whole world has come under the umbrella of the United Nations. All the countries under the United Nations, including Muslim countries, have agreed that no country will attack another. According to accepted international standards, now only one form of war is considered lawful and possible and that is of a defensive nature.

Owing to various factors, it has, in practice, become impossible to follow the above mentioned course. Holding a chronological order to be an eternal order is possible only if we admit that the practical manifestation of the Islamic mission was possible only once in human history and that, now repeating the same order for a second or third time is not a possibility.

Another quite basic requirement is to define the mission of the Prophet of Islam as being exactly the same as that of previous prophets. Any interpretation of his mission which does not tally with the history of his predecessors must stand rejected without discussion. For all the prophets, including the Prophet of Islam, were sent to the world to fulfill one and the same mission.

Chapter 42 of the Qur'an tells us that "He (God) has ordained for you the faith which He enjoined on Nuh and which We have revealed to you, and which We enjoined on Ibrahim, Musa, and Isa (saying):

> *'Observe this faith and do not be divided in it.'*
> *Hard for the polytheists is that to which you*
> *call them. Allah chooses for the faith whom He*
> *will, and guides to it those that repent."*
> *(42:13)*

In this verse, which refer to some steadfast prophets of the past, the Prophet of Islam has been enjoined by God to follow the same single religion, and strictly refrain from following a different path, for it is same religion which has been given to all the Prophets, including Muhammad. At another place, the Qur'an, mentioning a number of Prophets, who came at various places and in different periods, states:

> *"Those were the men whom Allah guided.*
> *Follow then their guidance." (6:91)*

According to this verse, all the prophets were guided in the same way as the prophet of Islam. That is why the prophet of Islam was to discharge the duties of his mission just as the other Prophets had done.

According to Qur'anic observations, only that concept of the Prophet Muhammad's mission could be appropriate which is fully in accordance with the mission of the other prophets. For all the prophets had been sent to fulfill the same mission. Granted this, any interpretation of his mission which presents it as being different from that of the other prophets can never be right.

For instance, if anyone were to say that, for the fulfillment of the prophet's mission, fighting and war were essential, this statement would not be correct. For the element of fighting is absent in the history of most of the prophets mentioned in the Qur'an. Similarly, if it were said that the Prophet of Islam did not accept any office under a non-Muslim political system, because accepting such an offer would have been an un-prophetic action, such a statement would not be right. For it is established by the Qur'an that the Prophet Yusuf did accept an office under an idolatrous king—an office which in today's jargon would be that of a minister of agriculture.

It may also be established from a study of the Qur'an that all the prophets were given the same religion. Yet their respective histories shaped themselves differently, for history has always depended on the prevailing sets of circumstances. As such, a correct appraisal of the teachings of the

Prophet would be that they have the status of the basics of religion, whereas the history that unfolds, as compared to the fundamental teachings of the religion, has the status of only a relative part.

When we study the Qur'an, in order to understand the prophetic mission, the clearest picture we have is one that occurs at four places in the Qur'an. At one place it is in the form of Abraham's prayer (2:129), and at other places it is found in general terms. While stating the purpose of sending the Prophet to the world, the Qur'an has this to say:

It is He who has raised among the unlettered, a Messenger from among themselves to recite to them His revelations, to purify them and to instruct them in the scriptures and wisdom, though they have hitherto been in gross error (62:2).

This verse fully explains the duty of the Prophet in this world as God's Messenger. A prophet has, essentially, four tasks as described in this verse. All other things that we find in the life of a prophet are incidental. The four things mentioned in the verse are relevant to the very mission of the Prophet, while all the other things besides these four relate to the historical circumstances in which the Prophet found himself. And it is a known fact that the reason for sending a prophet is in principle always the same, but in the course of his discharging this responsibility, the history that unfolds is never uniform; for it always varies according to circumstances.

The first step is the recitation of the verses, to the *madu*. This means the general communication of God's religion. The first and foremost duty assigned to a prophet was to convey God's message to people, all the while observing every form of etiquette in demonstrating wisdom and well-wishing for the *madu*. He was to bring people abreast of the creation plan of God which in the Qur'an is referred to as 'leading people out of darkness into light.' (5:17)

But the recitation of the verses did not mean that the Prophet had to recite the entire Qur'an to the people. For although this task began at the outset of his prophethood, at that time the whole Qur'an did not exist in the compiled form as it does today. What the recitation of verses meant was the communication of the basics of religion—that is monotheism, prophethood and *shariah*. The action of *dawah* is, in actual fact, a means of keeping people abreast of the basics of religion, whereas the detailed commands of the *shariah* are addressed to those who are already initiates, and not to those who have not yet entered the fold of Islam.

Another part of the prophetic mission was that which in this verse is called *'tazkia'* (purification). The act of purification meant the same as what is called instruction in present times. That is, man's thinking and feelings should be so reformed that he should be enabled to follow the path of God whole-heartedly and with total concentration.

The goal of the *dayee* in reciting the scriptures is to make people realize their ignorance and to convince them of the veracity of his message by putting forward cogent arguments. The goal of the Prophet in purifying people was to translate their *thinking* into action (those who had accepted the teachings of Islam were enabled to act accordingly) to awaken their spiritual feelings and to inculcate in them the real spirit of moral elevation.

The third part of the prophetic mission is described in the Qur'an in terms of teaching the divine book to the people. The instruction of the divine book meant an explanation of the commands and laws of the *shariah*. For instance, in the first stage people were asked to say: "God is one and He alone deserves being worshipped." In the second stage an attempt was made to inculcate the true spirit of worship. Later they were told what the practical form of worship was and how the etiquette of worship had to be observed.

The instruction of the book is also an education in *fiqh* (law). What is known as Islamic jurisprudence began with the Prophet himself. When people accepted Islam, they asked the Prophet to explain the commands of Islam on different matters. When the Prophet answered their queries, he was actually training them in law. This task of instruction in *fiqh* continued during the period of the Prophet's companions and the companion's companions. But it was not until the reign of the Abbasids that all the material on Islamic jurisprudence was properly compiled.

The fourth part of the prophetic mission is that which is described in the Qur'an as instructing in wisdom.

According to a tradition, the Prophet of Islam said, "Every verse of the Qur'an has a deeper level as well as a surface level."

What is called the deeper level of the Qur'an in this *Hadith* refers to the wisdom enshrined in the verses of the Qur'an. The wording of a verse or Hadith tells us only the apparent or superficial meaning. The deeper meanings are hidden behind the words, not in the words. These hidden meanings can be learnt only by deep reflection upon the verses. One task of the Prophet, therefore, was to initiate proper intellectual training, so that they might not only learn the apparent meaning of religious teachings but also understand the wisdom behind them.

The ability to exercise *ijtihad* on religious matters is also the result of this instruction in wisdom.

Those who are endowed with this deep insight are able to lead their lives on a high level of faith on the one hand, and on the other, they are able to discharge the responsibilities of the leadership of the *ummah*. Their mental faculties are so developed that they are able to make a proper interpretation of religion in the changing sets of circumstances.

In the above-mentioned verses we have been told that there are four aspects of the prophetic mission. Apparently this does not include certain parts of his life, such as *hijrah,* war, victory, the implementation of commands, etc. What is the reason for this? Why are these elements not included in the verses quoted above?

The reason is that the mission of the Prophet and the history of the Prophet are not identical. All those things which are not included in these verses form part of the history of the Prophet rather than of his actual mission. His mission was only one and the Prophet had always to fulfill it at all costs. No prophet could ever leave the world without fulfilling his mission. So far as the history of any prophet is concerned, this keeps changing according to circumstances. Various factors are responsible for changes in circumstances. That is why the history of each prophet is differently shaped despite all of them having had one and the same mission.

The actual status of the Prophet of Islam was that of a *dayee.* The Qur'an repeatedly presents him in this capacity:

> *'O Prophet, truly We have sent you as a witness, and a bearer of glad tidings and a warner, one who shall call men to Allah, by His command, and guide them like a shining light.' (33:45-46)*

These verses go to prove that the mission of the Prophet of Islam, far from being the establishment of political rule, was essentially *dawah.* It is true no doubt that in his life there were components other than *dawah,* but only that explanation of these other parts would be correct which did not affect his status as a *dayee.* Therefore it would be right and proper to say that the Prophet of Islam was in actual fact a *dayee.* Other constituents of his life were not direct goals, but rather became integral to his life due to extraneous factors.

The Prophet as a Model

The Prophet of Islam not only presented God's religion theoretically, but also diligently followed it in practice. Therefore, he is not only one who has told us what to do, but is also one who has demonstrated a practical example of what he preached:

> *'Truly, you have in the Prophet of Allah an excellent model for him who fears Allah and the Last Day and who frequently remembers Allah.' (33:22)*

This verse was revealed in the context of the battle of Ahzab. However, according to the principle of exegesis, it has a general application. As regards its general sense, this verse means that not only in the context of the campaigns of Ahzab, but in every respect, the Prophet's life serves as the best example for the believer. God's true servant is one who adopts the model presented by God's Prophet throughout his life.

A good or an excellent example does not mean a complete model as is generally understood. That is to say, it does not mean that from every aspect of human existence, all kinds of paradigms are to be found in the prophet's life. Rather it means that as regards principles he demonstrated fully in his practical life, those moral values which are regarded as being the best for human beings to practice. In that sense his is the ideal example to follow.

Yet it should not be expected that the Prophet's life will afford a list from A to Z of all the possible situations in which a model may be found necessary. No single person's life can cover such a broad spectrum of practical or ethical issues.

For instance, in terms of an "A to Z" list, one can say that the Prophet's life does not provide an example of normal family life with both parents alive, but does provide an example of orphanhood. The Prophet's life provides an example of how to bring up daughters, but does not provide an example of how to give proper training to sons. Similarly, one can say that we can learn from him how to wage war with arrows and swords, but not with guns and missiles. We may find examples in his life relative to the pre-scientific or traditional age, but there is no direct example in his life for things pertaining to the scientific age.

The life of the Prophet of Islam is indeed a perfect example. But this perfect example concerns principles rather than their application. The Prophet of Islam brought to the world high principles of ethics. He lived his life in complete accordance with these principles and set a practical example in his resolution of the issues and problems faced by him. In this way he became the best model for all human beings. However, this model enshrines principles, but not practical details. For instance, when he presented the model of a businessman, it related to being honest and not to how to organize business either in ancient times or in the age of computers.

It should also be taken into consideration that the Prophet's example does not relate to all human situations, but rather to certain basic matters. For instance, we find that the Prophet held some eatables lawful, and others unlawful, enjoining us to eat the lawful and forbidding us to eat the unlawful. On the other hand, in the context of the incident of pollination, the Prophet observed: 'You know your worldly matters better.' (*Sahih Muslim bi sharah an Nawawi* 15/ 118). That is to say that in areas such as horticulture, people are free to follow the method they find useful in terms of their research and experience.

Now let us look at this matter from another aspect. The above-mentioned verse of the Qur'an means that we must adopt whatever example we find in the life of the Prophet and follow that in our own lives. But on closer inspection, we find that it is not a simple matter.

The life of Muhammad as a Prophet was 23 years in duration. During this period, we find many diverse, rather opposite examples in his life. For instance, when he was in Makkah, he said his prayers secretly, but thirteen years after he reached Madinah, he began praying publicly. In the Makkan period, for a span of 13 years the Prophet remained aware of the idols placed in Kabah, but he never attempted to destroy them. It was only after the conquest of Makkah, (after being away in Madinah for 10 years) that he ordered the removal of all the idols. In the Makkan period, he used to recite to the people only those verses concerning the concepts of monotheism, hell and heaven, but in the Madinan period he gave practical commands on different aspects of life. In the Makkan period the Prophet made the Kabah his direction for prayer, but when he reached Madinah, he made the *Bait al-Maqdis* in Jerusalem his *qibla* (direction) for a period of sixteen months. In the Makkan period, the Prophet did not establish the system of congregational prayer, but when he reached Madinah, he built the first mosque and established the system of congregational prayer, etc.

Now the question arises as to how these different and apparently contradictory examples have to be followed. It is quite clear that all these examples cannot be followed at the same time—in following one example, some other example has to be abandoned. For instance, the life of the Prophet set the example of patience and circumspection as well as of war and confrontation. Now it is not possible to follow both examples at the same time. Whenever one is opted for, another shall necessarily have to be abandoned.

If we were to take our moral inspiration only from the latter stage of the prophetic life and ignore the former stage, this stand would certainly not be right. For, the entire 23-year prophetic life of the Prophet rather than just the final period, serves as an example for us. Making such a division in the life of the Prophet is patently wrong, not only in terms of the *shariah,* but also as a matter of reason.

In many verses of the Qur'an revealed in Makkah, God commanded the believers to follow the Prophet. For instance, in chapter 7, God commands:

> *Say 'People, I am sent forth to you all by Allah. He has sovereignty over the heavens and the earth. There is no god but Him. He ordains life and death. Therefore, have faith in Allah and His Apostle, the Unlettered Prophet, who believes in Allah and His word. Follow him so that you may be rightly guided.'* (7:158)

This verse and other similar verses go to show that the thirteen year period of the Prophet's life spent in Makkah is in all respects to be followed.

It is as good an example as that of the Madinan period. There is no difference between the two in so far as their being good examples is concerned.

This is an extremely serious matter requiring deep reflection. For instance, if one says that *jihad* is the sole solution to all communal problems, this assertion will not be true in its absolute sense; such statements negate all other examples of the Prophet, where he did not opt only for the way of *jihad*, but rather followed the path of patience and *hijrah*.

Similarly, if it were to be said that the goal of the Muslim *ummah* is the establishment of a complete Islamic system, such a statement likewise would not be right, for it would amount to a cancelling out of the entire life of the Prophet prior to the Last Sermon. As we know, several Islamic commands were finalized only on the occasion of the Last Pilgrimage. Neither had these commands been given previously nor had the revelation of the Qur'an been completed by that time. In such a case 'the good example' would amount to claiming that only the last phase of the Prophet's life served as a good example, at the time when the Qur'an was completed.

Giving the above interpretation to this verse, "This day I have perfected your religion" (5:3) is wrong both from the point of view of the *shariah* and of reason. The truth is that the entire Prophetic life, and not just a part of it, serves as an excellent model for us. Of all the examples it affords, none is either undesirable or to be discarded.

There are some who say that the whole matter of the Prophet's example is one of gradation. That is to say that the final goal of the Prophet of Islam is the one we find in his final phase after the last pilgrimage. That is to say, all the earlier examples are only those of initial stages, going by the principle of order and gradation, and not of the final and complete stage. This interpretation too is quite wrong, for there are statements in the Qur'an which clearly refute this theory.

For instance, the Qur'an tells the Prophet of Islam to follow the way of Ibrahim (16:123). As we know, the Prophet Ibrahim did not give his people a complete *shariah* in the sense of a comprehensive list of commands. His entire life was concentrated on the call of monotheism. Examples of the implementation of social commands or the establishment of the state do not exist in his life at all. In such a situation, according to the above-mentioned interpretation, this means that a prophet who has brought the complete *shariah* is being asked to follow a prophet who brought an incomplete *shariah*.

Similarly, after mentioning several prophets, the Qur'an says to the Prophet of Islam:

> "Those were (the men) whom Allah guided.
> Follow then their guidance (6:90)."

This statement of the Qur'an proves that the prophets mentioned therein were not bearers of the 'complete shariah' according to the above-mentioned interpretation, but rather had such basic teachings as that of monotheism, moral teachings, revealed to them. In such a situation if the above-mentioned interpretation is taken to be right, this would amount to saying that a bearer of the 'complete shariah' is being asked to follow the bearers of an 'incomplete shariah.'

Implementation According to Circumstances

The truth is that each one of the diversity of examples, found in the 23-year prophetic period, enjoys the position of a good example. Each example is perfect in itself. On the count of desirability, no one example is better than any other.

The reason is that according to the established principles of the *shariah,* man is obligated to observe the precepts of religion in terms of the actual circumstances he finds himself in, rather than in terms of some supposed goal (2:286). That is to say that the objective of Islam is not to set some external target, like the establishment of the perfect Islamic system, as an absolute.

According to this interpretation, the meaning of the verse about the 'good example' is that all the examples set by the life of the Prophet are equally worthy of being followed. That is, one has to study the life of the Prophet and follow to the letter that example which is applicable to his own particular set of circumstances. The Prophet had to face many kinds of situations. In this respect the Prophet's life offers examples for a great variety of circumstances. Now God's servants have to strive to find parallel examples and on finding guidance from his life, they must follow it wholeheartedly.

The contradictory examples in the life of the Prophet, are generally regarded as a matter of abrogation, for instance, when the verses on *qital* (to do battle) were revealed, the command to exercise patience and to practice avoidance was abrogated. But any absolute concept of abrogation is erroneous. Abrogation of one set of commands, opening the way to applying another set of commands, is relative to circumstances, and as such is only of a temporary nature. Whenever the circumstances change, the abrogated command may again become the more desirable one, in which case it will be observed just as it had been, previously.

For instance, on the occasion of Badr (2 AH) the Prophet acted on the command of war instead of on the command of *sabr* (patience). He came out of Madinah and did battle with the idolaters at a place called Badr. But on several other occasions the Prophet adopted a patient attitude in response to the armed aggression of the idolaters. For instance, on the occasion of Ahzab (5AH) in the face of the idolaters' military challenge the Prophet stayed in Madinah and, by digging a long trench, successfully prevented the idolaters from advancing. Thus by adopting this strategy, no actual fighting could take place. This clearly demonstrated an attitude of patience, which obviated *qital* or fighting.

Similarly, for instance, the Prophet said his prayers secretly during the first half of his stay in Makkah. But when he had migrated to Madinah, he began saying his prayers publicly.

The change of *sunnah* does not mean that now and for all time only the latter *sunnah* is applicable to the believers, and that praying secretly has been disallowed forever. Rather, according to circumstances, both the ways are equally desirable. When the circumstances are those of the Madinah period, the *sunnah* of the Prophet applicable to us would be that of public prayer. While the circumstances are those of the Makkah period, the same way of prayer which the Prophet adopted in Makkah would be applicable to the believers. From this analysis one can form a correct idea of all the other examples set by the Prophet Muhammad (may peace be upon him).

It should be kept in mind here that of all the prophetic examples, none is either superior or inferior, perfect or imperfect, eternal or temporary in nature. Each example to be found in the life of the Prophet is in itself a good example. Each example is equally a desirable *sunnah* of the Prophet. Given all these different *sunnahs*, the practice of any one of them, according to a particular situation would amount to total adherence to the Prophet's ideals. Provided the follower is sincere, he will be deserving of a full reward from God.

According to the above division, every set of *sunnah* is a complete *sunnah*, and following any set of *sunnah* is to follow the complete *sunnah*.

The believers are urged in the Qur'an:

> *"O you who believe! Enter into Islam wholeheartedly." (2:208).*

According to this verse, total submission to Islam is required of every believer. But total submission does not mean that all the commands have to be followed at the same time. Nor does it mean that we should launch a campaign to bring about the implementation of the total Islamic system. This verse simply means that we must wholeheartedly obey the command of Islam which we find is addressed to us in our particular situation. We have to show no hesitancy or lacking on our part in following that command.

For instance, if we find ourselves in such circumstances as make it possible to perform our prayers freely, it will be incumbent upon us to say our prayers properly when the time of prayer comes. Similarly, when believers find themselves in circumstances where they have freedom to engage in *dawah* work, it will be incumbent upon them to fully devote themselves to discharging the relevant responsibilities. Employing all the necessary means, they must perform *dawah* in the best possible way. Similarly, if circumstances permit them to enjoin good and forbid evil, individually or collectively they must strive to stop people from following evil ways. In such circumstances, all Muslims would be required to discharge this responsibility according to their capacity, and so on.

To sum up, total 'submission' relates not to the complete list of divine commands but to those particular and specific commands which from the point of view of the *shariah* are applicable to believers according to the situation in which they find themselves. There are so many comands in Islam but all these commands are not required to be followed in their totality, rather the application of these commands depends upon circumstances. This means to follow fully and wholeheartedly whatever command is applicable to a particular situation rather than trying to obey at thes same time each and every command enshrined in the Qur'an.

The Finality of Prophethood

According to Islamic belief, the chain of prophethood came to an end with the Prophet Muhammad (Peace be upon him), he being the final Prophet. No prophet is now going to be sent to the world by God. This is repeatedly mentioned in the Qur'an and *Hadith*. There is a specific verse to this effect in the Qur'an:

> *"Muhammad is not the father of any of your men. But he is the messenger of Allah and the seal of the prophets. And Allah has full knowledge of all things." (33:40)*

The word 'seal' (in Arabic *khatam*) as used in the above verse signifies a means of complete closure. (It should not be confused with 'stamp' which is something affixed to a document to guarantee its authenticity). The Prophet Muhammad being the 'seal of the Prophets' means that his advent put a stop to there being any continuation of the chain of prophets.

Abdullah Yousuf Ali, a well-known commentator on the Qur'an writes: 'When a document is sealed it is complete and there can be no further addition. Thus the prophet Muhammad put an end to the long line of Messengers. There has been and will be no Prophet after Muhammad. Thus when something is sealed, it is finally closed: nothing will come out and nothing will go in.

There are many traditions to this effect, a few of which we reproduce here:

> *"Messengership and Prophethood have been severed. Now there will be no Messenger and no Prophet after me."* (Ahmad, Tirmidhi).

> *"I came and I brought to an end the chain of prophethood"* (Muslim).

> *I am the last comer, there is no prophet after me* (Bukhari, Muslim). *I am Muhammad, the unlettered prophet and there is no prophet after me"* (Ahmad).

All these traditions have been collected by Ibn Khatir, a commentator on the Qur'an (*Tafsir ibn Kathir,* vol. 3, pp. 493-94)

Besides the verse mentioned above in Chapter 33, there are several verses which indirectly prove that there would be no other prophet and that there was no need for the advent of any other prophet according to the divine scheme. Here is another verse on this topic:

> *"The unbelievers have this day despaired of (vanquishing) your religion. Have no fear of them: fear Me. This day I have perfected your religion for you and completed My favour to you. I have chosen Islam to be your faith."* (5:3)

'Today I have perfected your religion' means that God has sent all the commands required by human beings. Here the perfection of religion is not referred to in the absolute sense. Rather it refers to the completion of the Qur'an as revealed to the Prophet Muhammad over a period of 23 years. Thus it is the completion of the revelation which is mentioned here, and not the completion of Divine Religion. That is why the wording is not 'Today I have completed religion,' but, 'This day I have completed your religion for you." The truth is that God has given His religion to man in a perfect form in every age. God has never given man an imperfect religion.

The community of believers in the Qur'an has been made by God to stand on such a solid foundation that it has the potential, to remain safe from all external dangers. Now, if it is ever to be harmed, it will be by its own internal weakness and not by external attacks or other dangers. The only guarantee of remaining free from internal weakness is that its members always go in fear of God.

In this verse 'perfection of religion' does not refer to the comprehensiveness of its rendition by the Prophet. That is to say that it does not mean that all the possible commands relative to all walks of life have been revealed to the final Prophet. In this verse 'the perfection of religion for you' means not the completion of the commands but the consolidation of religion. That is, now the religion of God is based on solid foundations. This consolidation is so perfect that it has risen above all enemy plots, and will not be harmed by them. From now until Doomsday, no antagonistic moves will ever affect it. The commentator An Nasafi has explained this verse as follows: "I have completed your religion" means that God had made the believers secure from the fear of enemies. He had given them dominion over the disbelievers. It is just like the kings saying that today "our power has been consolidated. That is, we are now secure from our enemies." (*Tafsir an Nasafi*, 1/270)

This verse is an indirect declaration of the finality of prophethood. A new prophet comes when the religion brought by the previous prophet is not preserved in its original form, that is, when the world is deprived of true guidance from God. Now when the consolidation of religion has become a guarantee that no plot or antagonistic move can distort the original form of God's religion, then in this situation there is no need for the arrival of a new prophet.

In more recent times, some self-styled claimants to prophethood arose and produced new religions, for instance Bahaullah (d. 1892) and Mirza Ghulam Ahmad Qadiani of India (d.1908). The argument common to all these self-styled prophets was that since times had changed, humanity had passed from the traditional age to the scientific age, or from the handicraft age to the machine age, and therefore the need had arisen to give man fresh guidance in view of the changed circumstances. On the basis of this thesis, they claimed that God had made them prophets to fulfill that need, and had revealed His words to them.

This argument is wholly baseless and irrelevant. It is, of course, true that with the aid of the latest technology, many changes have been made in modern times which have affected the course of civilization. But all these changes have nothing to do with revelation or prophethood. These words of the Prophet: 'You know your worldly matters better.'' (*Sahih Muslim bi sharah an nawavi,* 15/118) are applicable to the ways and means of daily existence.

God's prophets came to tell us of the principles that govern life. They did not come to guide us as to how to develop our civilization. Therefore, advancing arguments to prove the need for a new prophet with reference to cultural progress is quite futile. It has to do neither with *shariah* nor with reason.

Sir Zafarullah Khan, a *Qadiani*, has written a book in English in support of *Qadianism*. He believed that Mirza Ghulam Ahmad was a prophet of the modern age, holding that since the modern world had changed considerably, a new prophet was required to give people guidance, and that Mirza Ghulam Ahmad had come to meet this need.

This argument is nothing but a fallacy. The advent of a prophet does not relate to the changes of the times; it is meant rather to rectify the distortion or non-existence of the divine scriptures. If the world keeps changing, what is required is to re-interpret the divine religion according to the altered circumstances. And this task of re-interpretation is performed by religious scholars (*ulama*) and *mujtahids* (one who may exercise *ijtihad*). Therefore, no new prophet is required for this task.

As we know, the Qur'an exists even today in its perfect, original state. Not even minor changes have occurred in its text, and when God's word in the form of the Qur'an is preserved, there is no need for the coming of a new prophet.

One aspect of this issue is that the modern claimants to prophethood share the common viewpoint that one of the problems created in the industrial age is that of the pluralism of society. Communications having now greatly improved throughout the world, people adhering to different religions have felt encouraged to settle abroad, thus creating multi-religious societies in many countries. This is a new state of affairs, one with very few precedents. It is maintained that while commandments may exist in Islam for a uni-religious society, there are none for a multi-religious society. This situation, it is claimed, necessitates the advent of a prophet to tell us the divine commands regarding this problem.

The solution to this problem offered by latter day claimants to prophethood was that truth is found in all religions, as alluded to in this verse of the Qur'an:

> *"And it is surely mentioned in the scriptures of the former peoples." (26:197).*

They held that since truth was to be found in all religions, the adherents of one religion must believe in other religions, just as they believed in their own religions.

But this is not a problem for the solution of which a new prophet is required who would bring new commands. Indeed, the answer to this question is found in the *sirah* of the Prophet himself. When the Prophet migrated to Madinah from Makkah, at that time Jews and idolaters too lived there alongside the Muslims. Madinah's society, in effect, was multi-religious in character.

At that time the Prophet of Islam issued the "Charter of Madinah." This Charter, establishing the administrative leadership of the Prophet, declared that the affairs of each religious group would be decided according to its own religious and tribal traditions. This gives us the principle that a multi-religious society should be organised in a way that the central administration rests largely in the hands of the majority community, while each religious or cultural group will enjoy the right to organize its internal matters according to its own beliefs and traditions.

Again, the problem of producing a peaceful atmosphere in a multi-religious society is not a religious issue in itself. It is a different matter altogether. It is not true that if each religious group considered that other religious groups possessed the truth, the desired peace would ensue. The most important factor in bringing about a peaceful society is rather the feeling of tolerance. A society which nurtures tolerance will be one in which tranquillity reigns, whereas a society without this quality will be split by dissension.

History tells us that an atmosphere of conflict exists equally in uni-religious and multi-religious societies. For instance, the battle of the Mahabharat took place between two groups of Hindus. The second world war took place between Christian countries. In Afghanistan, a bloody war is taking place between two groups of Muslims, and so on. To put it briefly, the secret of social peace lies in mutual respect and not in mutual recognition.

Thus this problem is not one of common belief but rather of common respect–respecting the adherents of all religions. This is the solution we have been given to this problem in Islam.

Of the many verses in the Qur'an which relate to this issue of the finality of prophethood, the following is of particular significance:

> *Pray during the latter part of the night, an additional duty (for which) your Lord may exalt you to a position of praise and glory. (17:79)*

(A 'position of praise and glory' is translated in Arabic as *Muqam-e-Mahmood'*). One aspect of this exalted station pertains to this world and another to the Hereafter. This is called by the commentators The Great Recommendation (*shafa'at*). As we find from the traditions, on the Day of Judgement all the prophets will testify to the sincerity of faith of their followers, then they will be ushered into heaven–for they are, indeed, the ones whom God wants to be sent to heaven. The believers thus vouched for by the Prophet of Islam will be the largest in number. The other, worldly aspect of his high station is that such historical glory has gathered around him that he has earned universal acclaim in the eyes of all the nations of the world. This was the plan of God which was completely fulfilled in his favour. Today the people of the world are compelled to acknowledge his greatness. His prophethood has become established, no longer being controversial as it was in the early years.

Exalted prophethood, from the worldly point of view is another name for established prophethood. In the case of the Prophet Muhammad, so many historical proofs exist that there is no room for any doubt as regards his personality and his teachings. Man by his own accepted academic standards is compelled to acknowledge his position. The ultimate form of recognition is praise and glory. That is why this position is called the *muqam-e-mahmood*.

This verse on *muqam-e-mahmood* was revealed in the second stage of the Makkan period at a time when Islam had not been consolidated. Later God made such changes in circumstances that the religion of Islam in every respect became perfectly consolidated. The Qur'an was so perfectly preserved that now there is no possibility of any changes, or interpolations in it, or of any additions being made. The *sunnah* or the traditions were compiled after the Prophet became an acknowledged historical figure. A vast community (*ummah*) and countless institutions and so on, were established to safeguard the religion of Islam.

When God's religion is so preserved and consolidated, it becomes possible even without the personal presence of the Prophet to fully understand God's religion and practice it. After such momentous events have taken place, as marked the life of the Prophet, humanity does not continue to live in the darkness of ignorance; it is brought into the light of knowledge. Thus for any seeker after truth it becomes not only possible but also easy to learn the will of God. And this is the reason for sending the prophets to the world. When this purpose is being served, there is no reason whatsoever to send another prophet.

Trusting Human Nature

During his 23-year movement, the Prophet Muhammad brought about a revolution which caused the entire political system of ancient times to be re-structured. But there was another event far greater than that and this took place at the level of human thought. People who had been idolaters prior to this revolution became monotheists; those who had been insolent became submissive, those whose thinking had been parochial became upholders of the international message; those who had known nothing but fighting and aggression became champions of peace and humanitarianism, spreading their message all over the world; those who had had no history of their own, rose to fashion a history of the nations of the world.

Now the question arises as to how the Prophet succeeded in bringing about this unique revolution. Again the answer is that a huge amount of sacrifice was needed to bring it about. This sacrifice is what in today's jargon we call as 'taking risks'. But the world is governed by the principle: the greater the risks the greater the success. Changing human beings is the most difficult task in this world. Therefore, one who aspires to do so cannot but imperil his own interests. As far as this world of cause and effect is concerned, the Prophet Muhammad took the greatest of risks, and hence the success he achieved was also the greatest.

Here we present two examples to illustrate this point. The first example concerns the conquest of Makkah. The majority of the Makkans at the time of its conquest were still idolaters. These were the same people who had displayed the greatest antagonism towards the Prophet and his companions. They had expelled him and his companions from their homes. They had waged offensive battles against him. They had killed a large number of his companions and had made several attempts on his life. Their crimes were so great that the only fitting punishment according to the prevalent custom was to have all of them beheaded.

Their past crimes could be forgiven, but another danger lurked which was even greater: if these people were set free, they might reorganize themselves to plot against Islam and once again wage battles against the Muslims.

All these people were brought to the Kabah, the

house of God. They stood there as if on the verge of death. But, instead of awarding punishment, the Prophet declared a general amnesty for all of them, saying, "Go, you are all free." When the Prophet took such a great risk, he benefited equally as a result. This was setting an example of trust in human nature, although it had its dangers.

As a narrator puts it: "After this unexpected general amnesty, when these opponents came out of the House of God, they felt as if they had come out of their graves. And then all of them entered Islam." (*Hayat Al Sahaba* 1/175)

When these people came to the Prophet Muhammad, after the conquest of Makkah, they were in a psychological state when death seemed certain; they felt sure that they were to be consigned to their graves. The moment the Prophet granted them pardon, it seemed as if they had been given a new lease of life. It was such a great favour to them that after this they could no longer remain obdurate, and psychologically it was no longer possible for them to remain insolent after such noble behaviour on the part of the Prophet. Ultimately, they all embraced the religion of the Prophet. The very people who had been the greatest of enemies now became his greatest companions and supporters. This is the most unique event in history, but this could come about only because the Prophet dared to take the most unique risk.

Another noteworthy incident which took place after the conquest of Makkah concerns the Hawazin tribe. The Prophet and his companions, heading for Taif by a route bordered by Hawazin settlements, avoided encounters with the tribesmen and did not so much as utter a word of criticism against them. Yet, when they were half way along the floor of a valley running through Hawazin territory, the tribesmen rained down arrows upon them from the hill tops. At this sudden onslaught, the Muslims were stricken with panic. Many precious lives were lost. However, after an initial defeat, the Muslims won the battle. About 6,000 people were taken captive.

These prisoners of war, according to the prevalent custom, deserved the severest of punishment. Furthermore, their release again posed a severe threat to Islam. In this respect arriving at a decision to set them free was undoubtedly taking a great risk. But the Prophet of Islam did take this risk and liberated the prisoners without setting any conditions. They were even provided with mounts and provisions so that they might comfortably travel to their homes.

Again the same miracle happened. They converted to Islam en masse. The truth is that the extraordinary magnanimity of the Prophet rid them entirely of their haughtiness.

There was no other path that they could have opted for: they had to accept the religion of the Prophet. Old enemies were now turned into friends.

In fact, if the deeds of the Prophet of Islam were to be subtracted from history, such examples would be eliminated, where not only the external political structure is transformed but also the very innermost recesses of human beings.

One important part of the *sunnah* of the Prophet of Islam is trust in human nature. We find examples of his following this principle throughout his entire life.

Man is not a statue made of stones. Rather he has a precious gift within him in the form of human nature. This nature is the most important part of a human personality. This is what is referred to in the Qur'an in the following verse:

> *"By the soul and Him who propotioned it and inspired it with its impurity and purity."*
> *(91:7-8)*

This shows that everyone by birth wants to know what is good and what is bad; what is wrong and what is right. This means that the *dawah* about to be presented by the *dayee* is already vaguely or unconsciously known to the *madu*. Therefore, when the *dayee* issues to man the call of truth, it is as if it is a known message for the *madu* and as if the *dayee* is trying to bring the message to the *madu* from the unconscious to the conscious.

This fact gives the *dayee* conviction that the message he is going to deliver to the *madu* had already been inculcated in his nature from the time of his birth. The *madu,* by his own inner nature, is compelled to acknowledge the truth. The realization of this fact saves the *dayee* from frustration. He is able to ignore the apparent recklessness or opposition on the part of the *madu* and continue to present the message with the conviction that, one day or another, the *madu* will certainly welcome his words of wisdom.

The *dawah* life of the Prophet of Islam is replete with examples of such conviction and confidence. In spite of apparent antagonism, his conviction was never shaken, that one day or the other the hearts of his hearers would be opened and their human nature would be compelled to accept the message.

That is the reason why, in spite of the worst opposition, he never cursed people who were apparently his enemies. Instead he always prayed for them. For instance, when Tufayl Ibn Amr Ad Dausi came to Makkah and accepted Islam, he was sent by the Prophet to his tribe to give them the call of *Tawhid.* Far from listening to him, they *tormented* him. Tufayl again came to the Prophet and said to him: 'O Prophet, my tribe, the Daus has become an oppressor. So curse them.' But the Prophet did not curse them. Instead he raised his hands and prayed in these words: 'O God, give them guidance.' (*Seerah Ibn Hisham* 1/409).

After praying for them, the Prophet asked Tufayl to go back to his tribe and deal with them gently, in spite of their hardness towards him, and to be their well-wisher and speak to them reassuringly. The Prophet gave this advice, for he was convinced that the Daus tribe was no exception. They were also human beings like the others. They were also invested with the same God-given nature as others had. And it turned out that the Prophet had rightly trusted human nature. When Tufayl went back to his people and called them again to the call of monotheism, the miracle happened. Gradually all the men and women embraced the call of the faith of monotheism. Trust in human nature is a great *sunnah* of the Prophet of Islam, and we find examples of it in every stage of his life.

In the Madinan period when the call of Islam spread all over Arabia, delegations from different tribes in and around Arabia started coming to the Prophet and accepting Islam. One such incident of this period concerns the tribe of *Thaqif.* A delegation from this tribe came to Madinah in 9 AH. The Prophet of Islam conveyed to them the teachings of Islam. They were ready to accept Islam, but they insisted on many conditions being met. They said that they would say prayers, although it was an act of humiliation, but they would neither pay charity nor perform *jihad.* In spite of all these conditions, the Prophet accepted their oath of allegiance and admitted them into the fold of Islam.

Certain Muslims had reservations about this kind

of conversion, but the Prophet said: After they have accepted Islam, they will pay charity as well as perform *jihad* (*Seerah ibn Kathir*, 4/56).

If the Prophet of Islam had concentrated only on the utterances of the people of Thaqif, he would not have accepted their Islam. But the Prophet had full trust in human nature. Instead of seeing them in terms of the present, the Prophet saw them as they would be in the future. His estimate was proved entirely right. The people of *Thaqif* took no time in accepting and practising all Islam's teachings willingly and wholeheartedly.

It was a result of this policy that the Prophet never felt the need to resort to violence against opponents. He treated his enemies as if they were his friends. That is why for the first time in human history he was able to bring about an almost bloodless revolution throughout the whole nation.

The Qur'an tells us that God created all human beings with the same nature. "And follow the nature made by Allah—the nature in which he has created mankind. There is no altering the creation of Allah." (30:30).

This same point has been made in a *Hadith* in these words: "Every child is born according to nature." (*Tafsir ibn Kathir*, 3/432)

There is another *Hadith* to this effect: "God has created human beings with an upright nature." This shows that all human beings are born with the same nature. There is no person in whom enmity to the truth has become an inseparable part of his nature.

From the *dawah* point of view, this is an extremely important reality. It means that if the *dayee* finds that some people are his antagonists and others his friends, then he should not consider this difference to be a real one. Trusting the nature man is born with, the *dayee* must think along the lines that if some people are his direct supporters, others who appear to be antagonists are his potential supporters. This thinking gives enormous hope to a *dayee*. He nurtures in his heart the same well-wishing for his opponent as he feels towards his friend. He is able to address his apparent enemies cool-mindedly, and without losing his balance, until the time comes when his enemies turn into his friends. This is the reality pointed out in the Qur'an:

> And good and evil are not alike. Requite evil
> with good, and he, between whom and you is
> enmity will become your warm friend. (41:34)

An enemy becoming a friend does not mean that earlier he was fire, then he became water. The truth is that he was water already, only some superficial layers had obscured his true personality. The *dayee* manages with his unilateral good behaviour to remove these superficial layers. After that the real man within comes out. And, at the level of the real, inner personality, every human being is predisposed to truth. No one is averse to it as far as his nature is concerned.

The Prophet of Islam availed of the services of non-Muslims many times in his life. After the death of Abu Talib, when he was deprived of the patronage of his tribe, he approached different tribes to seek their support, in spite of the fact that they were idolaters. Then after his return from Taif, he managed to enter Makkah once again under the patronage of Mutim ibn Adi, a leader of an idolatrous tribe. In his journey to Madinah, he chose a *mushrik* (idolater) Abdullah ibn Urayqit as his guide. There are many such incidents of this nature, which show that the Prophet repeatedly trusted non-Muslims and sought their help. Dividing people into friends and enemies is against the *sunnah* of the Prophet and against human nature as well.

A study of *seerah* shows that trusting human nature is a permanent principle of Islam. According to Islam the words uttered by people, or even their activities, are not worthy of great consideration. For all these things are ephemeral. While dealing with people, the actual factor worth considering is human nature. Man is basically subordinated to the temperament he is born with. All other things are only of a temporary nature. They do not enjoy the position of a decisive element in the matter of human behaviour.

This *sunnah* of the Prophet shows that in both

individual or social affairs, we must always ignore superficial factors. It is the demand of human nature which has to be given the greatest importance and making concessions to it is a sure guarantee of all kinds of success.

If an individual or a group becomes provoked, then this provocation is not worthy of real consideration. What should be considered is that, despite apparent provocation, man's nature should continue to remain unchanged.

In such a situation, if we are able to give concessions to human nature by avoiding provocation, problems will ultimately solve themselves. The provocation will vanish on its own and then what will be left will be the element of humanity, which is the nature with which God created us.

Studying the Prophet's Life in the Light of his Message

The present age is regarded as being fraught with difficulties for Islam. But the actual state of affairs is quite the opposite. In fact, Islam has done for the present age what the annual monsoon rains do for agriculture.

But Muslims, because of their lack of awareness, have failed to understand this and as such have not been able to turn Islamic potential to good account.

What is called religious ascendancy in the Qur'an was not of a temporary nature, but was rather a proclamation of the eternal domination of Islam. This meant that, in the world of ideology, such a revolution would take place as would lead to Islam remaining in the forefront forever. Such potential is produced by God, but the task of putting it to the proper use falls on the believers.

The aim of the revolution brought about by the Prophet and his companions in the 7th century was the dominance of divine religion as enshrined in the following verses of the Qur'an:

> *"They seek to extinguish the light of God with their mouths; and God refuses to do otherwise than perfect His light, although the infidels may abhor this. It is He who has sent down His Messenger with guidance and the true faith so that He may make it prevail over all religions, even though the idolaters may dislike it." (9:32-33)*

What is meant here by ascendency (in Arabic, *izhar*) in the religious context is ideological and not political pre-eminence. It follows that from the doctrinal standpoint, God's religion will assume such a superior position that ideological veracity will become the sole preserve of Islam.

Granting ideological ascendancy to divine religions is no simple matter. It is, in fact, akin to producing an entire new history. As a matter of fact, God's religion has always enjoyed a superior position, but since ancient times, human sciences and learning had been evolving along superstitious lines. This had cast a veil over its pristine state.

Now God ordained that such an ideological revolution should be brought about by the Final Prophet as would transform this unfavourable, man-made situation. After this had taken place, the human sciences themselves would testify to the truth of divine religion. By the accepted academic standard of human beings, the religion of monotheism would be proven authentic.

In the above verse, the predominance of religion was to result from a divine plan carried out with the succour of God by the Prophet and his companions. And indeed, this revolution initiated a new process in human history. Its aim was to unravel all superstitious veils in order that all such hidden scientific proofs might be revealed as would highlight the truth of the religion of monotheism. This revolution in modern times has reached its culmination.

There were two chief objectives of this predominance of religion. One was to bring the system of religious coercion to an end, so that the task of *dawah* – a task which had to be performed in the past in very difficult circumstances–could be performed in a propitious atmosphere. The other aim was to lend the full support of rational argument to God's religion, so that no other religion could compare with Islam in terms of ideological veracity. These two tasks have been performed on a large scale in modern times. We give below a brief description of this.

In ancient times the rule of monarchy was prevalent all over the world. Such a system, based as it was on personalities, could be upheld only by force. That is why kings everywhere had resorted to coercion to establish and maintain their positions, inevitably crushing any tendency towards intellectual or religious freedom. This state of affairs was a permanent obstacle to performing *dawah* as well as to the general development of human thought. The aim of the revolution brought about by the Prophet and his Companions was to abolish the oppressive political system of the times and to usher in an age of freedom and democracy. This revolution gradually influenced the course of human history, and remained alive until in modern times it reached its culmination. Now calling people to accept religious truth can be done in total freedom. Earlier this task was seriously hindered by the atmosphere of oppression.

In ancient times polytheism (in Arabic, *shirk*) dominated the minds of people all over the world. Whole nations were so mentally fettered by superstitious thought that the development of science had become well-nigh impossible. The Prophet and his companions, however, put an end to the irrational beliefs arising from superstition. In this way they opened the doors to the scientific way of thinking and paved the way for the advent of the age of science. Now the scientific revolution of today has, in turn, opened up vast opportunities for Islamic *dawah*.

One result of this scientific revolution, which was, in fact, a by-product of the Islamic revolution, is our modern system of communications, which has made it possible for the first time in human history to perform the task of the propagation of Islam much more rapidly and on a world-wide scale. According to a tradition of the Prophet, a time would come when God's word would enter all the homes of the world (*Musnad Ahmad*). It is a prophecy, in an indirect sense, of the coming of this age of fast communications. For, without the modern media, the universal propagation of Islam could never have become so accelerated.

This modern scientific revolution has resulted in the development of a new, scientific rationale in support of Islamic beliefs. Earlier, *dayees* of Islam had only traditional types of arguments to draw upon. In present times it has, indeed become possible to authenticate Islamic realities by measuring them up to accepted scientific norms.

In ancient times, religion was considered sacrosanct, so that any study of it could only be uncritical.

That is why, academically, no distinction could be made between reliable and unreliable religions. In present times, under the influence of the scientific revolution, religion has begun to be treated in the same objective and critical manner as other non-religious matters and subjected to the same scientific scrutiny.

This has established on a purely intellectual level that, historically, Islam is the only reliable religion.

All other religions are lacking in this historical credibility. It was only after this intellectual awakening that it became possible to verify the truth of Islam by the standards of pure human knowledge, and to advance arguments for its being, out of all the religions, the only true religion.

These modern developments have brought Islam to the point of unopposed victory. Now the need of the hour is for Muslims to end unilaterally all activities characterised by hatred and violence against their *madu* nations, so that normal relations may be established between *dayee* and *madu* and Islam may be communicated to them in strife-free circumstances.

There is now the possibility of initiating a serious and fruitful dialogue between Islam and non-Islam. Undoubtedly the results of such efforts will be in favour of the former.

A Great Potential

Since direct argument is not possible so far as religious beliefs concerning the unseen world are concerned, only indirect or inferential argument can be applied in order to prove their veracity. This fact had led the scholars to believe that religious realities were a matter of beliefs alone; they were not scientific truths. But in present times, after the smashing of the atom, a revolution has taken place in the science of logic, and now it has been admitted that inferential argument too is, in essence, as valid as direct argument. Subsequently, it has become possible to establish religious realities at the same scientific level on which proofs (or disproofs) are offered for material or non-religious theories.

In ancient times when man looked at the world, he would see that apparently there was in existence a great variety of objects so different from each other as to seem at times to be almost the opposite of one another. This observation produced the mentality of *shirk.* People thought that if things were diverse, there should also be a diversity of creators. But scientific studies have shown that this difference, or diversity, is only on the surface. Otherwise all things have originated from the same matter. This discovery deprived the *shirk* of any scientific basis, while scientific findings established an intellectual basis for monotheism.

According to the statements of the Qur'an, the signs of God lay hidden in the heavens and the human mind. Scientific studies brought them to the knowledge of the people (41:53). Ultimately, the universe assumed the form of a great book of divine arguments.

With the new discoveries of science, many things have come to light as have made it possible to use new arguments to establish realities which are of religious importance. For instance, carbon-14 dating has made it possible to specify the exact age of the body of Ramses II (Moses's contemporary) so that the following Qur'anic statement could be scientifically verified:

"This day We shall save your body, so that you may become a sign to all posterity." (10:92)

Islam and the Modern Age

Islam is a religion of peace, in the full sense of the word. This being so, the question arises: Can Islam, which offers the teachings of peace, be relevant for the modern age? Can it regain a superior position for itself in changed circumstances?

The answer is totally in the affirmative. The very fact of Islam being a religion of peace shows that it is an eternal religion. If it had been otherwise, it would not have endured. For in this day and age, according to modern thinking, the use of violence has been totally rejected. Now the human mind finds acceptable or worthy of consideration only that system the teachings of which are based on peace and non-violence.

Communism, for example, has been rejected by modern thinking. One of the major reasons for this was that the proponents of communism believed in violence. And under no circumstances can the modern mind find this acceptable. Other ideologies like Nazism and Fascism have already been rejected on the same score. If modern man dislikes religious or secular extremism, it is because this leads ultimately to violence.

Islam, however, is a religion of nature and has always been an upholder of peace. For this reason violence and extremism have been held totally undesirable from day one. For human construction, Islam has played a great role as a result of which human history entered a new phase of progress and development. The time has come today for Islam to play its constructive role once again and lead human history into a new phase of progress.

What is known as scientific or technical progress is the result of the discovery of nature. This nature has always existed in our world, so why has its discovery been so delayed? Why could the scientific progress made over the last few centuries not have been made thousands of years ago?

The reason was that in ancient times religion and science (divine learning and human learning) were inextricably linked with one another. In this way religious dogma was a permanent obstacle to scientific development. What Islam did was to separate religion, which in those days was nothing but a set of superstitious beliefs, from the process of scientific investigation. For instance, lunar eclipses and solar eclipses were believed to affect human destiny. The Prophet of Islam declared that eclipses had no bearing on the fate of human beings, for all such events were astronomical in nature and unrelated to the human lot. (*Fathul Bari* 2/611)

This separation of religion and science is ably illustrated by the well-known incident of the pollination of dates which was narrated by Musa ibn Talha on the authority of his father and recorded in the *Sahih* of Imam Muslim:

I was with the Prophet when he passed by some people who had climbed up to the top of some date palms. The Prophet enquired as to what they were doing. He was told that they were pollinating the trees in order to fertilize them. The Prophet said, 'I don't think this will benefit them.' When people learned of the Prophet's comment, they stopped the practice of pollination. The yield, however, was very low that year. When the Prophet came to know of this, he said, "If they benefit from pollination, they should continue with this practice. I had only made a guess and formed an opinion. There is no need to follow my opinion in such matters. If, on the other hand, I say anything about God, it must be adhered to. Because I never say anything untrue when I am speaking of God."

The Prophet's advice amounted to delinking religion and science. In this way scientific research found an atmosphere of freedom in which to advance. Subsequently, for the first time in human history, scientific knowledge began to develop without the intervention of religion, and gradually reached the present stage of its development.

Today, once again, man is faced with a more serious impasse. That is, despite extraordinary progress in science and technology, human life is beset with all kinds of problems, and there appears to be no sign of getting rid of them.

This modern dilemma, in brief, is the unwillingness to recognize that freedom should have its limits. Modern man hailed personal liberty as the summum bonum, but failed to set boundaries to it. Therefore, freedom became akin to permissiveness, which can lead only to anarchy. All the afflictions of western society today are traceable to this. Now man requires an ideology, which specifies distinct areas of freedom, and draws the line between desirable and undesirable actions. Only Islam can provide this kind of ideology.

Today the time is ripe for people to open their hearts to Islamic ideology. For one thing, the fall of communism has produced an ideological vacuum which Islam alone can fill.

In the present world, we have countries which are economic super-powers and military super-powers. But the place of the ideological super-power remains vacant, and that belongs, potentially, to Islam alone. There is only one obstacle to the realization of this potential and that is Muslim movements having taken a violent course in present times. These movements present Islam to the world in the guise of a violent religion. That is why modern man shies away from it. He develops a bias against it. But when this prejudicial state of affairs is brought to an end, and Islam is presented to the world as a non-violent religion, with a peaceful ideology, once again humanity will welcome it with open arms.

There is no religion of this kind today except Islam. It is Islam and Islam alone which meets all human needs. Individually, there are many men and women who, having studied Islam, have acknowledged its very special qualities. Out of these, some acknowledge the virtues of Islam in the ideological sense. Others have gone further and accepted Islam as a total way of life.

Dawah Activism

Islamic activism, in respect of its method, is based on non-violence, and in respect of its goal, on *dawah*. *Dawah*, in fact, is another name for the peaceful struggle to propagate Islam. It would therefore be true to say that Islamic activism and *dawah* activism are synonymous.

The work of *dawah* is no simple task. It enjoys a pivotal position. When this work is performed with thoroughness, all other difficulties will automatically be overcome. On this subject the Qur'an has this to say:

1. If we perform *dawah*, God will protect us from all evil-doers. (5:67)
2. *Dawah* turns enemies into friends (41:34)
3. *Dawah* proves the ideological superiority of Islam.

And without doubt there is nothing greater than ideological superiority.

4. *Dawah* produces positive thinking among the *ummah* which, in the Qur'an, is called 'honest counsel'. (7:68)

5. The task of *Dawah* is done through human beings, but conducive conditions for its performance are provided by God Himself—just as the rains are sent by God, but the work of cultivation is to be performed by the farmers. Now it is the duty of the believers to refrain from squandering their energies on fruitless activities. They should instead devote all their efforts to *dawah* work. All the best results will follow.

When, his life under threat, the Prophet of Islam left his native Makkah along with 200 of his Companions, the Makkan leaders having made their lives unbearable the very first speech he made after reaching Madinah was quite remarkable in being untinged by bitterness or threats of revenge on or retaliation against the Makkans. (*Seerah* ibn Hishain, Part II, p. 118-19)

On reaching Madinah, he attached the utmost importance to entering into peace negotiations with the different tribes around Madinah, e.g. the Banu Khuza'a. These peace agreements were to the effect that neither would they (the tribe) fight against them (the Muslims) nor would the Muslims fight against them. Most of the Arab tribes entered into these peace agreements.

But the Quraysh of Makkah insisted on maintaining an aggressive stance, and even made some hostile moves as well. Finally, in the sixth year of *Hijrah,* the Prophet succeeded in resolving matters by a peace agreement reached at a place called Hudaybiya. However, this agreement with the Quraysh was made by unilaterally accepting their conditions.

Islam is a peace-loving religion in the full sense. If others create an atmosphere of violence and disharmony, the demand of Islam on such occasions will be to refrain from retaliatory violence and avoid reaction. Such positive steps are to be taken as will enable peace to be established between the Muslims and non-Muslims.

The reason for this is that the aims Islam wants to promote can be realized only in a peaceful atmosphere. In the negative atmosphere of violence and confrontation, no target can be achieved.

That is why the Prophet of Islam always unilaterally exercised patience. Whenever others wanted to ignite the fire of hatred and violence, he adopted such strategies as might, by God's guidance, bring about an atmosphere of mutual love, toleration and moderation.

Whenever they kindle the fire of war, Allah puts it out. (5:67)

In the context of the position of ascendancy assumed by Islam in the early days, Muslims are duty bound to continue their struggle in this direction, from generation to generation, so that the religion of Islam may always enjoy a superior position.

This is a non-political goal and can be achieved only through non-political means. Only that movement is right for the achievement of this goal, which takes up Islam purely ideologically and confines this struggle to a purely peaceful sphere.

The Power of Peace

Non-violent activism, which should not be confused with passivity, is the perfect solution to problems in all spheres.

Whenever any problem arises between two groups, be it individual or social, one way to deal with it is to opt for the way of violence and confrontation. Another method is to make every attempt, by scrupulously avoiding the path of clash and confrontation, to solve the problem by peaceful means. There are many forms which peaceful means may take; it is, in fact, the exact nature of the problem which tells us which of the peaceful means is to be employed on which occasion.

Islam teaches us non-violence. The Qur'an tells us that God does not love disorder (2:205). This verse also clearly states what is meant by disorder. According to the Qur'an, disorder is that course of action which results in disturbance in the social system incurring loss in terms of life and property (2:205).

We may put it differently and say that certainly God loves non-violence. He does not want people to indulge in such violence in human society as would result in death and destruction. This is also supported by other statements in the Qur'an, one of which tells us that one of God's names is *As Salaam*, meaning Peace (59:23). Similarly, God's desired religion is called 'paths of peace' (5:16). Paradise, the ultimate destination of God's true devotees, is called the 'home of peace' (6:127).

The entire spirit of the Qur'an is in tune with this concept. For instance, the Qur'an attaches the greatest of importance to patience. Patience is the only Islamic act which is promised reward beyond measure (39:10). Patience, in fact, is another name for peaceful activism, while impatience is another name for violent activism. Patience, in essence, is exactly what is called non-violence in modern times. Patient activism means non-violent activism.

This point has been clearly made in the *Traditions*. According to one Tradition, the Prophet of Islam observed: God grants to non-violence what he does not grant to violence. (*Sunan abi Dawood* 4/255)

In this tradition the word '*rifq*' (gentleness) has been used as compared to '*unf*' (violence). These words denote exactly what is called violence (*unf*) and non-violence (*la unf*) in modern times. It bespeaks the eternal superiority of non-violence over violence.

God grants to non-violence what he does not grant to violence. This is no simple statement. It tells us of a very profound reality. It tells us of an eternal law of nature. By the very law of nature itself, all bad things are connected with violence, while all good things are connected with non-violence. Violent activities breed hatred in society, while peaceful activities breed love in society. Violence is a source of destruction, while non-violence is a source of construction. Hostility flourishes in an atmosphere of violence, while amity flourishes in an atmosphere of non-violence. The way of violence gives rise to negative values, while the way of non-violence gives rise to positive values. The way of violence embroils people in problems, while the way of non-violence shows people the way to exploit opportunities. To put it briefly, if violence is death, non-violence, as compared to violence, is life.

Both the Qur'an and *Hadith* speak of *jihad* as a very superior act. What is *jihad*? *Jihad* means 'struggle.' This word is used for non-violent activism as compared to violent activism. One clear proof of this is provided by the verse of the Qur'an which says:

> *"Do not yield to the unbelievers, but struggle with them by means of it (the Qur'an) most strenuously." (25:52).*

The Qur'an is no gun or weapon of war. It is a book of ideology. In such a situation asking people to struggle by means of the Qur'an signifies to strive by means of ideology. That is to say, to work hard to conquer people's hearts and minds by the superior ideology of Islam.

In the light of this Qur'anic explanation, it would be true to say that *jihad*, in fact, is another name for peaceful activism or non-violent activism, that is to say, if *qital* is violent activism, *jihad* is non-violent activism.

Peaceful Beginning

When the Qur'an began to be revealed, the first word of the first verse was *iqra*, 'read.' (96:1) When we reflect on this verse, we find the starting point of Islamic action. It is to start from where there is no fear of violent reaction, from the point where it is possible to continue one's movement along peaceful lines.

At the time when the command of *iqra* was revealed in the Qur'an, several options existed in Makkah regarding the starting point for the Islamic movement. One option was to begin by launching a movement to clear the Kabah of the 360 idols which had been placed in it. This option would certainly have provoked a violent reaction on the part of the Quraysh. Another option was to find a seat in *Dar Al Nadwah* (Makkah's parliament). The third option was to launch a movement to free Muslims from the domination of the Roman and Sassanid empires.

This starting point again would have provoked a violent reaction on the part of these forces.

Leaving aside all these courses of action, the option followed was that of studying the Qur'an, about which it was certain that it could be continued peacefully, and that it would not provoke any violent reaction.

The Prophet of Islam adopted this principle throughout his life. His policy was to adopt a non-violent method rather than a violent method. It is this policy which was referred to by his wife, Aisha: "Whenever the Prophet had to opt for one of two things, he always chose the easier one."

The Benefits of Non-Violent Activism

What are the advantages of non-violent activism over violent activism? These are listed here in brief:

1. According to the Qur'an, each human being is endowed with two faculties: the ego, which is called *nafs ammara* (12:53) in the Qur'an and the conscience, which is called *nafs law wama* (75:2).

   Violent methods arouse people's egos, which inevitably results in some form of destruction. Conversely, non-violent activism awakens people's consciences, which results in introspection in the people concerned. This brings about miraculous results and, in the words of the Qur'an, the enemy becomes "your dearest friend." (41:34).

2. One great benefit of the non-violent method is

that people's time is not wasted. In this way they have the occasion to exploit the opportunities existing in the prevailing circumstances to the ultimate extent. We find this in the case of the no-war pact of Hudaybiya. This peace treaty made it possible for the energies of the believers to be expended in peaceful constructive activities rather than being wasted in armed confrontation. (*Seerah* ibn Khathir, 3/324).

3. One tremendous harm resulting from violent activism is the breaking of social traditions in order to launch such movements, whereas the great benefit of non-violent activism is that it can be continued without any disruption of tradition.

4. Violent activism ultimately destroys the existing system, for the replacement of one system by another is not possible by this means. On the contrary, through non-violent methods it becomes possible to gradually replace one system with another. That is why movements based on violence end up by bringing about one political coup or another. True revolution cannot result from any movement launched on the basis of violence.

Success Through the Non-violent Method

All great successes or victories in the first phase of Islam and in the succeeding period were achieved by the non-violent method. Here we refer to some of these victories.

1. The first thirteen-year period of the prophethood is called the Makkah period. The method of non-violence, or pacifism, was adopted in the full sense in this phase. Many issues which presented themselves in Makkah could easily have led to confrontations. But the Prophet of Islam, avoiding all such issues, confined himself totally to the sphere of the peaceful propagation of 'the word of Allah.' It was as a result of this policy that *dawah* work in this period could be effectively performed. One of the many benefits of this 13-year *dawah* work was that in this age all the best individuals who influenced Islamic history were brought into the fold of Islam, for instance, Abu Bakr, Umar, Usman, Ali, etc.

2. When the Makkan leaders wanted to wage war against him, the Prophet, declining to retaliate, quietly migrated to Madinah.

   Hijrah, in its nature is without doubt an example of non-violent activism. This peaceful strategy enabled the Prophet and his migrant companions, about 200 in number, to build a powerful centre of Islam in Madinah. If the Prophet had opted for the way of armed confrontation instead of peaceful migration, perhaps the history of Islam would have begun and ended in Makkah.

3. After the emigration, the Prophet's antagonists waged war unilaterally. The outcome was the

bloody pitched battles at Badr and Uhud. At that moment, the Prophet again negotiated a 10-year peace treaty by accepting all the conditions of the enemy. This pact is known in the history of Islam as the Hudaybiya peace treaty. This event is called a 'clear victory' in the Qur'an (48:1). It was this peace pact which paved the way for that peaceful constructive activity which finally made possible the conquest not only of Makkah but the whole of Arabia.

4. At the end of the pious Caliphate, a bloody confrontation between the Banu Hashim and the Banu Umayyah took place. As a result, the advancement of Islam came to a halt for ten years. What re-opened this chapter of advancement was the retreat of Hasan ibn Ali (d. 50 AH) from the field of battle. This step was indeed a practical form of non-violent activism. This peaceful step taken by Hasan ibn Ali once again opened the doors of progress to Islam.

5. By the end of the Abbasid caliphate, Mongol tribes had attacked the Muslim world and destroyed the entire region right from Samarqand to Aleppo. Apparently the history of Islam had come to a standstill. At that juncture Muslims had engaged in peaceful *dawah* work. As a result, the majority of the Mongols accepted Islam. How that miraculous feat occurred was expressed by an orientalist in these words: "The religion of Muslims

has conquered where their arms had failed."

6. Another important event of this nature concerns the scholars of Islam of the early phase. After the pious Caliphate, the political set-up had degenerated. The Caliphate had permanently changed into kingship, and apparently there had been developments that invited confrontation with the rulers. But according to the guidance of the Prophet, the believers totally avoided political clashes with those in power. A history of political corruption, starting from the time of the Umayyad caliphate, continued for centuries. Yet the great religious scholars known as *tabiin*, the disciples of the Prophet's Companions, *taba tabiyiin,* companions of the *tabiin,* the traditionists, the jurists, the *sufis,* all the great religious scholars, refrained without exception, from setting themselves on a collision course with the rulers.

It was no simple matter to avoid the field of violent activism and opt for the field of non-violent activism. It was during this period, therefore, that on the one hand, peaceful *dawah* work was initiated in various countries, and on the other, the Qur'an, *hadith, fiqh,* and other Islamic sciences were compiled. All the precious books of classical Islamic literature that adorn our libraries owe their existence to this peaceful course of action.

For instance, *Hadith* is regarded as the second source of *shariah* after the Qur'an. These traditions, having been compiled, are available to us in the form of books. These are so precious that, without them, the very structure of religion could not have taken shape. During the respective reigns of the Umayyads and Abbasids, when the rot had set in in the rulers, most of these traditions were retained only in the memories of the traditionists of the times. Had these traditionists opted for the principle of violent collision with the oppressor-rulers of their time, all of them would have been done to death by the rulers. Then all the precious treasures of traditions, instead of becoming parts of the books, would have been lost to posterity.

It is the miracle of the choice of non-violence over violence that the precious treasure of the traditions is available today in printed form on our bookshelves. We are thus in a position to fully benefit from the guidance given to us by the Prophet.

Political Insurrection Unlawful

After the period of the pious Caliphate, corruption set in in the Muslim rulers. Still the religious scholars did not rise in revolt against the rulers, scrupulously avoiding any confrontation. They continued to expend their efforts in non-political fields. This was not simply a matter of chance but the adoption of a policy based on the clear injunctions of the *shariah*. As we know, books of *Hadith* record the traditions in detail under chapters like *al-Fitan* (Trial).

The Prophet had clearly foretold that in later times all kinds of rot would set in in the rulers. They would become tyrants and unjust, but even then the people should never take up arms against them. Instead the Prophet advised that when the believers found themselves being ruled by such tyrants, they should take to the mountains with their 'camels and goats' instead of launching campaigns against them.

'Camels and goats' signify those opportunities which existed in non-political fields, and which will always exist irrespective of the corruption of the rulers. The Prophet's injunction meant that at such times what the believers have to do so is to peacefully exploit the existing opportunities in non-political fields by avoiding any confrontation in the political field. These injunctions of the Prophet were so clear that the religious scholars formed a consensus that, staging an insurrection against the rulers was unlawful, and therefore to be totally avoided in all circumstances.

In the commentary of Sahih Muslim, Imam an Nawawi, commenting on the traditions in the chapter 'Al-Imarah', writes: "Do not adopt the way of confrontation with the rulers in the matter of their power. If you find them going against Islam, you should try to make the truth clear to them by sincere counselling. So far as launching campaigns and taking up arms against them to oust them from positions of power is concerned, that is unlawful by the consensus of Muslims, even if the ruler is evil and a tyrant (*Sahih Muslim bi Sharh an Nawawi,* 12/229).

This injunction of the Prophet of Islam, as made clear above, was based on extremely important considerations. The truth is that in the first phase (and in later phases as well) a large number of academic, *dawah* and reform works outside the political field, had to be performed. Without this, the very history of Islam, would have remained incomplete, for if the religious scholars had engaged themselves in confrontation with the political institutions, all these constructive activities could never have been carried out. Therefore, the Prophet of Islam gave express commands to avoid political confrontation with the rulers at the slightest pretext. This avoidance served as a guarantee that all the constructive activities outside the field of politics would continue uninterruptedly.

In every society two parallel systems exist side by side—one political and the other non-political. The latter governs a variety of institutions which function independently of politics. According to the scheme of Islam, the non-political system established at the social level has to be always kept stable; all believers are expected to do their utmost to ensure that despite changes, rot or corruption in the political set-up, Islam should be firmly established on a non-political basis.

The Command of War in Islam

Certain verses of the Qur'an give the command to do battle (22:39). Here are a few points on this subject that we learn from our study of the Qur'an.

1. The first point is that to initiate aggression or armed confrontation is absolutely forbidden for Muslims. That is why the Qur'an clearly states: Fight in the cause of God those who fight against you, but do not transgress (2:190).

2. Islam allows only a defensive war. That is, when aggression is resorted to by others, Muslims may engage in war only in self-defence. The initiation of hostilities is not permitted for Muslims. Combat may be engaged in only when "they (the opponents) were the first to commence hostilities against you." (Qur'an, 9:13)

   Furthermore, even in the face of aggression, Muslims are not immediately to wage a defensive war. Instead they are to employ all possible means to prevent a carnage from taking place. They are to resort to fighting only when it becomes totally unavoidable. All the battles that took place during the life of the Prophet provide practical examples of this principle. For instance, during the campaign of Ahzab, the Prophet attempted to avoid the battle by digging a trench, and thus successfully averted war. If, on the occasion of Hunain, the Prophet had to engage in battle, it was because it had become inevitable.

3. There was another kind of war, according to the Qur'an, which was temporarily desirable. That was the struggle to end religious persecution (*fitna*) (2:193).

In this verse '*fitna*' refers to that coercive system which reaches the extremes of religious persecution. Prevalent all over the world in ancient times, this system had effectively closed the doors to all kinds of spiritual and material progress for man. Therefore, God commanded His devotees to put an end to the kings' and emperors' reign of terror in order to usher in an age of freedom in which man might receive all kinds of spiritual and material benefits.

This task was undertaken internally within Arabia during the life of the Prophet of Islam. Afterwards, the Sassanid and Byzantine empires were dismantled by divine succour during the period of the rightly-guided caliphs. Consequently, the coercive political system ended at the international level, and thus began an age of intellectual freedom.

In this connection we find a very authentic tradition recorded in Sahih al-Bukhari. When, after the caliphate of Ali ibn Abi Talib, Abdullah ibn Zubayr and the Umayyads engaged themselves in political confrontation, Abdullah ibn Umar (son of the second Caliph) and the seniormost surviving companion of the Prophet kept himself aloof from this battle. A group of people came to him and, referring to the verse (2:193), which commanded the believers to do battle in order to put an end to persecution, asked him why he was not willing to join the battle, Abdullah ibn Umar replied that *'fitna'* did not refer to their political confrontation, but referred rather to religious persecution, which they had already brought to an end. (*Fathul Bari*, 8/160).

This makes it clear that the war putting an end to persecution was a temporary war, of limited duration, which had already been concluded during the period of the rightly guided caliphs. Now justifying the waging of war by citing this verse is not at all acceptable. This verse will apply only if the same conditions prevail in the world once again.

Biographers of the Prophet have put the number of war campaigns at 80. When a reader goes through these biographies, he receives the impression that the Prophet of Islam during his 23-year prophetic period waged wars at least four times a year. But this impression is entirely baseless. The fact is that the Prophet of Islam in his entire prophetic period fought only three battles. All the other incidents, called *ghazwa,* or military expeditions, are in fact, examples of avoidance of battle, rather than of involvement in battle.

For instance, the incident of al-Ahzab has been called a battle in the books of *seerah.* Whereas in reality, on this occasion, 12,000 armed tribesmen of

Arabia came to the border of Madinah in order to wage war, but the Prophet and his companions did not allow the battle to take place by digging a trench which acted as a buffer between the Muslims and the aggressors. The same is the case with all those incidents, called *ghazwa,* or battles. Whenever the Prophet's opponents wanted to involve him in battle, the Prophet managed to defuse the situation by adopting one strategy or another.

There are three occasions when the Prophet entered the field of armed combat–at Badr, Uhud and Hunain. But as proven by events, fighting had become inevitable on all these occasions. The Prophet had no choice but to do battle with the aggressors. Furthermore, each of these military engagements lasted for only half a day, beginning at noon and ending by sunset. Therefore, it would not be wrong to say that the Prophet in his entire life took up arms only for one and a half days. That is to say, of the entire 23-year prophetic period, except for one and a half days, the Prophet observed the principle of non-violence.

While giving the command of battle to the Prophet and his companions, the Qur'an clearly states that it was the other party which had commenced hostilities (9:13). This verse gives conclusive evidence that there is only defensive war in Islam. It is absolutely unlawful for the believers to wage an offensive war. The Islamic method is entirely based on the principle of non-violence. Islam does not allow for violence in any circumstance except that of unavoidable defence.

The Present Age and Non-Violence

The greatest problem facing Islam in present times, to my way of thinking, is that Muslims have consigned the *sunnah* of non-violence to oblivion. In more recent times, when Muslims faced such problems as that of Palestine, the fall of the Mughal empire, and the Turkish caliphate, they fell prey to negative reaction on such a large scale that they completely forgot that the policy of Islam was that of non-violence and not of violence. It is as a result of this deviation from the teachings of Islam that even after a 100-year long bloody war, there has been no positive outcome. The outcome has, in fact, been the reverse. They have lost to an indescribable and unimaginable extent what still remained to them after losing their empires.

According to Imam Malik, this *ummah* will be reformed in its last phase just as was done in its first phase. That is to say, that just as the issues of the first phase of Muslims were settled by the non-violent method, so will the issues of latter day Muslims be settled likewise. If a violent course of action did not yield any benefit in the past, neither will it do so in future. The circumstances of present day Muslims resemble those that prevailed at the time of

Hudaybiya. Today once again the unbelievers are guilty of bigotry (48:26).

The solution to this problem in the first phase lay in the Muslims' refusal to display bigotry by not falling prey to the psychology of reaction but rather adhering strictly to the path of *taqwa* (righteousness) since that would entitle them to divine succour and a clear victory (48:26).

The Quraysh, who enjoyed the position of leadership in Arabia, were bent on waging war at the time of the Hudaybiya treaty. The Kabah was in their possession. They had expelled the Prophet and his companions from their own homeland. They had taken possession of Muslims' homes and properties. They ceaselessly engaged in antagonistic activities against Islam.

Given this state of affairs, the Muslims had two options before them. One, to wage war with their opponents in the name of putting an end to persecution and securing their rights. This option would certainly have resulted in further loss in terms of lives and resources. The second option was to exercise patience on the question of political and material loss for the time being and to exploit the opportunities that still existed. The Prophet of Islam and his companions chose the second option. The result was splendid: within just a few years the history of the whole country underwent a revolution.

Prophetic Guidance for the Modern Age

The Qur'an tells us that the Prophet of Islam was sent as "a mercy for all mankind" (21:107). There is nothing mysterious about this. It is a natural reality which can be understood by making an academic and rational study of it.

When a human being is born, he finds himself in a world which is astonishingly vast and complex. How man has to relate himself to his world and how he has to form his ideas are matters of which he is totally ignorant. Neither is his birth accompanied by a guidebook, nor does he find a board set up on some hill-top inscribed with the necessary guidelines which he is to follow.

That is why man continues to grope in the dark, finding only scraps of knowledge to lay his hands on.

Science and philosophy are two such cases in point. What is philosophy? Philosophy is an attempt to discover the secrets of the universe at the academic and scientific level. Man is born with a feeling of curiosity. Instinctively he feels the urge to find out the reality of things. That is why philosophy has always existed in rudimentary form since the very advent of man in the world. However, philosophy took a proper and organized form three thousand years ago in Greece. Subsequently in various academic and intellectual centres, philosophic discussions and debates were engaged in all over the world.

After a continuous effort for five thousand years, philosophy has not been able to give any meaningful concepts to man. During this long period of time the strivings of great minds have ended only in intellectual confusion and dissension (*intishar*). On the other hand, science gave man, within a period of just 200 years, so many new ideas that we find it difficult to enumerate them. It is science alone which has led man to the age of modern civilization.

What is the reason for this difference? The reason may be traced to the fact that science recognized the limitations of knowledge and, by accepting this reality, made full use of whatever knowledge it had at its disposal. But the case of philosophy was different. It remained ignorant of its limitations for thousands of years. In ancient times the fields of philosophy and science were not separate from one another. They were regarded as equal parts of human knowledge. Ancient philosophers considered all aspects of knowledge as belonging to their own sphere and gave thought to all of them in their totality.

Three hundred years ago the division of study was worked out, in that the subjects of science and philosophy were separated from one another. Now the perusal of realities of meaning or truths became the subject of philosophy, while the objective realities became the subject of science. That is to say, the chemistry of flowers became the subject of science while the meaningfulness of flowers became the subject of philosophy. This division of knowledge, or in other words, this acknowledgment of human limitation led to the emergence of extraordinary results. In ancient times, man remained engaged in intellectual efforts without differentiating between the knowable and the unknowable. This was a totally futile effort. But when he separated the unknowable and began working only on the knowable, then his efforts were crowned with spectacular success.

This is an instance which shows how important it is in this world to recognize intellectual limitations: efforts bear fruit when man accepts the boundaries of knowledge. Before launching himself on an any course of action, he should know the correct starting point. He must have a clear perception of the difference between what is knowable and what is not.

Only a keen realization of this distinction will yield appropriate results. A lack of proper understanding will render the greatest of efforts futile.

From this example we can understand how important to man is the guidance of God's Prophet. God is the Creator of the universe and as such is fully aware of its secrets. He then selects a person from amongst human beings, giving him all the fundamental knowledge which is necessary for construction and development. This is the divine guide, a prophet, whose advice makes it possible for man to begin his journey in a state of enlightenment, so that he may receive the blessings of both worlds.

Man has received many beneficial things from the Prophet of Islam. The first of these is conviction. It is the Prophet's guidance alone which enables man to begin his life with the full confidence of faith. Man is certainly in need of such knowledge as may guide him in his thoughts and actions. One discipline we turn to in this connection is philosophy. But philosophy itself admits that it has yet to reach the ultimate reality, for it is still in the questing stage. This being so, all that philosophy can give man is scepticism. It cannot provide him with a source of conviction.

Then comes science. But science has itself admitted its inability to perform this service, having declared in advance that its chosen subject of study was only a part or the outward face of the knowledge of the universe. Knowledge of the universe as a whole was not to be an object of scientific research. Obviously, science is too limited in scope to provide man with the intellectual gift called conviction.

The nineteenth century saw the rise of socialism, which acquired the status of a complete philosophy of life as expressed by the ideology of Karl Marx (d. 1883). This ideology, initially given wide credence, cast its spell over a large number of the world's intellectuals. In 1917, on the basis of this ideology, Marx's supporters established a full-fledged government in Russia, which later expanded to become a great empire– the Soviet Union. From that time right into the middle of the twentieth century, Marxist socialism was the dominant world ideology. The American economist, John Kenneth Galbraith, claimed that Marx himself had achieved greater popularity in present times than all other historical figures, including Muhammad. The Marxist magic was undone only when the Soviet Union itself disintegrated in 1991.

By the grace of God, about 35 years before the fall of the Soviet Union, by delving deeper into realities, I was able to come to the conclusion that Marxism as a philosophy was entirely baseless. After a detailed study of the subject, I wrote a book titled: *Marxism Tarikh jis ko rad kar chuki* (Marxism rejected by history), which was published in 1959 by Maktaba Islami, Rampur. Today everyone is aware that the charm of Marxism has evaporated, so that it is difficult to find as many as two individuals who receive from Marx such intellectual nourishment as will bolster confidence and conviction.

Next comes the turn of religion. What is religion? Religion in its reality is the name of that knowledge which has come directly from God. Knowledge has been divided into two categories in the Qur'an— experimental knowledge and revealed knowledge:

> *Bring me a Book (revealed) before this or some vestige of knowledge (in your support) if you indeed speak the truth (46:4).*

In principle it is true that religion is the source of truth and can bestow upon man the blessing of conviction. But here a historical reality has come in between men and religion. That is, none of these existing religions are historically credible. There are about one dozen major religions in the world, there being also countless minor religions. But there is no historical evidence to support their reliability or credibility.

Furthermore the revealed scriptures of these religions have been marred by human interpolation. This is a proven fact. There are many contradictions in their assertions. Purely academically, it is difficult to separate the human and the divine world.

When the image of religion was distorted by human additions, God sent His Last Messenger in order that he might put an end to discrepancies and tell man the truth.

This is the reality that has been pointed out in the Qur'an:

> *"We have sent down to you the Book so that you may explain to them that concerning which they differ and as a guidance and as a mercy for a people who believe" (16:64).*

The divine book given to the Prophet is a perfectly preserved book. As such, it serves as a reliable source of divine guidance and confers upon its readers the blessing of conviction that they have been seeking all along. Confidence and conviction are essential for the building of life in this world.

One highly important point in the construction of a healthy human society is that human beings should learn the exact nature of man and woman. In the present age of freedom, there has been a growing belief that men and women are equal in every respect. In fact, modern society is adhering more and more to the principle that both should play an equal part without any discrimination in all social activities.

But the pursuit of such a course has destablized human relationships to the point of throwing all social departments into disarray. The result is that in present times, despite extraordinary progress in civilization, man is not able to secure peace and contentment. There is no doubt about it that the most damaging factor is the acceptance of this modern concept of absolute equality between men and women. For details see the book titled: *"Women in Islam"* by the author.

In this matter, had man adopted the guidance given by the Prophet of Islam, he would never have suffered any lack of balance. One of the realities conveyed by God through the Prophet of Islam concerns the law of nature, viz. the creation of man and woman having been done in such a way that each of them has been given something which the other has not been given. In this way both go together to make a whole. Neither is complete in himself or herself. But when they both join together, a complete whole is produced.

This is the reality which has been thus expressed in the Qur'an:

You are the offspring of one another (3:195).

This finds expression in a *Hadith* in these words: Truly women are half of men (*Sunan abi Dawood,* 1/60).

One aspect of the knowledge that man receives from the Prophet may be called the divine scheme of things. That is, the Prophet tells us what is God's scheme in life for man and the universe. This is essential for an understanding of life on earth. Those who are oblivious of this reality can never make a successful plan in life. For instance, thinkers of modern times may have devised ideal plans for the building of society, but these have largely failed to contribute anything positive to humanity, because of the unnatural premises which these thinkers took as their point of departure, i.e. they envisioned a social system in which all sections of society would find an equal position.

When we judge this projection by the criterion of nature, we find a basic weakness in the underlying theory. The difference existing between men socially and economically is not in reality traceable to exploitation. Nor is it due to the plotting of tyrants. The real difference stems from the fact that people are born different. For instance, some are more intelligent, some are less intelligent; some are strong, some are weak; some find every opportunity to work, while others are faced with some accident or early death; some are born in favourable circumstances, while others live and die in penury.

This difference, created by nature itself, is largely the result of the different status of people in society. And this difference is related to external factors which are beyond human control. Then how can human beings ever root out these differences?

Socialist thinkers hold that all the resources of production should be taken over by the government so that it may enforce equality among all people by the use of state power. When the socialist system attempted to do so, it was revealed that this artificial effort to produce equality had killed something greater, and that was the incentive to action.

In the socialistic system no one was the owner; all were salaried government servants. This bid to bring about equality therefore eliminated the very thing which was the greatest incentive to action—that is personal interest. That is why progress and development in socialistic societies were affected to such a dangerous extent that they ultimately collapsed.

The truth is that the difference between human beings is not an evil but rather a great boon. It is this difference, in fact, that causes people to continuously face challenges and enter into competition in a free human society. Challenge and competition are stimuli which keep people perpetually active. A society which eliminates difference and disparity will also eliminate challenge, and in its absence human initiative will wither away. The Creator of all things has created this world for the purpose of putting human beings to the test. But the thinkers want to carve out a plan of life without taking this purpose into account. In any case, they have so far failed to formulate a plan, so the question of establishing a practical system does not even arise.

For instance, all these thinkers vehemently hold forth on sin and wickedness. They even go to the extent of saying that the greatest problem our human society faces in this world is the presence of evil. That is why we have to pay the utmost attention to this matter.

But this is unrealistic thinking. What these thinkers call the problem of evil is, in fact, a major factor in the exigencies of man's trial. Since this world has been created for the purpose of testing, many such incidents will inevitably take place as are mistakenly referred to as evils.

For instance, if the Creator of human beings desires to test them on the scales of patience and gratefulness, then it is essential that at times they should find themselves in difficult situations in order to see whether or not they remained patient on those occasions. Similarly, it is also necessary that man should receive the good things of life in order to see whether or not he responds with proper gratefulness or with insolence and haughtiness. Moreover, this purpose of man's stay on earth requires some to be given more and some less resources. This is to test whether those who are given less remain free from the evil feelings of jealousy, and whether those who are given more spend the money solely on their own luxury or on the service of humanity, etc.

In the modern age, freedom has been given the status of summum bonum. Its prevalence stemmed, in fact, from the general reaction to the coercive system established by the despotic monarchs of ancient times. Freedom is without doubt extremely precious so far as human progress is concerned. But unbounded freedom, on the contrary, results in disaster. In a hundred year experiment with unlimited freedom, thinkers are coming to the fore in the West who hold that freedom cannot be given the status of an absolute good. For instance, B.F. Skinner has written a book titled, *'We Can't Afford Freedom.'* The title indicates the gist of the book.

Through the Prophet of Islam, modern man is being shown how to differentiate between healthy and unhealthy freedom. The Prophet has brought real knowledge to the demarcation of what is lawful and what is unlawful. Similarly, through the Prophet of Islam, modern man can understand how to arrange for a practicable division of the workplace between men and women by according them equal respect. A knowledge of human limitations is essential for the proper organization of all matters in life. And man receives this knowledge of right and natural limitation only through a prophet.

This is the greatest boon of the Prophet to modern man: his teachings give man the opportunity to organise his life in a far better way, and on a far higher plane.

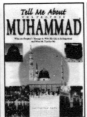

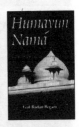

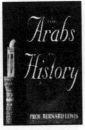

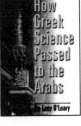

THE HOLY QUR'AN

The Pilgrimage to MAKKAH

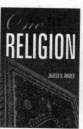

One RELIGION

ZAHEER U. AHMED

ISLAMIC THOUGHT

S. WAQAR AHMAD HUSAINI

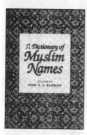

A Dictionary of Muslim Names

Edited by PROF S. A. RAHMAN

Ibn Battuta

H.A.R. GIBB

ISLAM REDISCOVERED

THE SPREAD OF ISLAM IN THE WORLD

A Historical Survey

Prof. Thomas Arnold

The Blessings of RAMADAN

Javed Ali

The Story of the Prophet Nuh

Quran Stories for Tiny Tots

THE STORY OF THE PROPHET YUSUF

Quran Astronomy

Earth Exploration from Space

Children's Stories from the Quran

The Ark of Nuh and the Great Flood Sticker Book

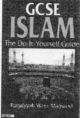

GCSE ISLAM

The Do-It-Yourself Guide

Ruqaiyyah Waris Maqsood

GOD ARISES

MAULANA WAHIDUDDIN KHAN

THE MORISCOS OF SPAIN

HENRY CHARLES LEA

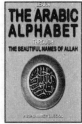

THE ARABIC
ALPHABET
THROUGH
THE BEAUTIFUL NAMES OF ALLAH

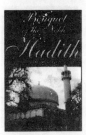

Forty
Hadith

On the
importance of
knowledge,
learning and
teaching

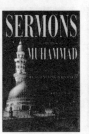

SERMONS
OF
MUHAMMAD

A HISTORY OF
ARABIC
LITERATURE

ISLAMIC ART
ARCHITECTURE

After Death,
Life!

Thoughts to alleviate
the grief of all Muslims facing
death and bereavement.

Introducing
Islam
A Simple Introduction to Islam

INDIAN
MUSLIMS

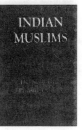

PRINCIPLES OF
Islam

THE MORAL
Vision

Tabligh
Movement

WORDS
OF THE
PROPHET
MUHAMMAD

SELECTIONS FROM
THE HADITH

HANDBOOK OF MUSLIM BELIEF

Islamic Thought and its Place in History

De Lacy O'Leary

THE MIRACLE IN THE ANT

HARUN YAHYA

THE MIRACLE OF CREATION IN PLANTS

HARUN YAHYA

THE MIRACLE IN THE SPIDER

HARUN YAHYA

Death Resurrection Hell

HARUN YAHYA

ALLAH IS KNOWN THROUGH REASON

HARUN YAHYA

TIMELESSNESS AND THE REALITY OF FATE

HARUN YAHYA

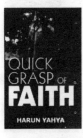

QUICK GRASP OF FAITH

HARUN YAHYA

THE MIRACLE OF THE IMMUNE SYSTEM

HARUN YAHYA

CRUDE UNDERSTANDING OF DISBELIEF

HARUN YAHYA

HARUN YAHYA

EVER THOUGHT TRUTH?

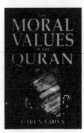

THE MORAL VALUES OF THE QURAN

HARUN YAHYA

ETERNITY HAS ALREADY BEGUN

HARUN YAHYA

The Basic Concepts in the Quran

HARUN YAHYA

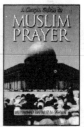

A Simple Guide to MUSLIM PRAYER